WHY THE ★★★★★ TURKEY DIDN'T FLY

PAUL ARON

The Colonial Williamsburg Foundation
Williamsburg, Virginia

in association with

UNIVERSITY PRESS OF NEW ENGLAND
HANOVER AND LONDON

© 2013 by The Colonial Williamsburg Foundation
All rights reserved. Published 2013.

24 23 22 21 20 19 18 17 16 15 14 13   1 2 3 4 5 6

Library of Congress Cataloging-in-Publication Data

Aron, Paul, 1956-
  Why the turkey didn't fly / by Paul Aron.
     pages cm
  Includes bibliographical references and index.
   ISBN 978-0-87935-261-5 (pbk. : alk. paper)
 1. Emblems, National--United States. 2. Signs and symbols--United States.
I. Colonial Williamsburg Foundation, issuing body. II. Title.

 JC346.A76 2013
 929.9'2--dc23

                     2012041839

 ISBN 978-0-87935-261-5 (CW)
 ISBN 978-1-61168-494-0 (UPNE)

Designed by Helen M. Olds and Shanin M. Glenn

Printed in the United States of America

Colonial Williamsburg® is a registered trade name of The Colonial Williamsburg Foundation,
a not-for-profit educational institution.

The Colonial Williamsburg Foundation
PO Box 1776
Williamsburg, VA 23187-1776
www.history.org

Published in association with University Press of New England

Contents

The Great Seal of the United States, lithograph by Andrew B. Graham (prob. 1885–1900). Library of Congress.

"I WISH THE BALD EAGLE had not been chosen as the representative of our country," Benjamin Franklin wrote in a 1784 letter to his daughter. "He is a bird of bad moral character. He does not get his living honestly. You may have seen him perch'd on some dead tree near the river, where, too lazy to fish for himself, he watches the labour of the fishing hawk; and when that diligent bird has at length taken a fish, and is bearing it to his nest for the support of his mate and young ones, the bald eagle pursues him and takes it from him." Franklin preferred the turkey, "a much more respectable bird, and withal a true original native of America." The turkey was a little vain and silly, he conceded, but "a bird of courage, and would not hesitate to attack a grenadier of the British guards who should presume to invade his farm yard with a red coat on."

How, then, did the eagle become our national symbol? For that matter, why did Gilbert Stuart's image of George Washington end up on the dollar bill? This despite the fact that Rembrandt Peale, an artist admittedly interested in promoting his own portrait of Washington, noted "the inaccuracy of its drawing and its deviation from the true style and character of [his] head." And why, despite the dearth of evidence, do we persist in teaching our kids that Betsy Ross sewed the first flag?

Preface

This book tells the stories behind the images of America that originated in the nation's early years. I hope you will find the stories amusing, and sometimes surprising. Perhaps, too, the stories of these images—of Yankee Doodle and Uncle Sam, of George Washington and Benjamin Franklin, of liberty bells and liberty poles and liberty trees—will shed some light on how Americans saw themselves and the nation they created.

The American Revolution, John Adams believed, was more than a war. "The Revolution was in the minds and hearts of the people," he wrote in 1818. The images in this book sprang from those changing hearts and minds, and they themselves changed many a heart and mind.

WHEN AMERICANS THINK of the Declaration of Independence, most envision a handwritten parchment with fifty-six signatures, most prominently that of John Hancock. Hancock wrote his name twice as large as that of any other signer. He did so, he supposedly explained, so that King George III "can read my name without spectacles." Whether Hancock actually said these words is highly questionable. Even more shocking to most Americans, the handwritten copy with the signatures, displayed under armed guard at the National Archives in Washington, D.C., is not the original document that the Continental Congress approved, and the Declaration was not signed on July 4.

The Continental Congress voted for independence on July 2, 1776, and two days later Congress did indeed adopt the Declaration. The document that Congress adopted that day, handwritten by Thomas Jefferson, has

Declarations

been lost (although an earlier draft, also in Jefferson's handwriting, has been preserved and is in the Library of Congress). In any case, according to most historians, the members of Congress did not sign any document on July 2 after the vote or on July 4 as most Americans assume. What Congress did do, having adopted the Declaration, was direct John Dunlap, its official printer, to set the words in type and make copies to send to the various states as well as to the commanders of Continental troops. These printed sheets were the first official copies of the Declaration. They were not handwritten and they, too, were not signed (though the text was followed by the words "Signed by order and in behalf of the Congress, John Hancock, President"). We do not know how many copies John Dunlap printed the night of July 4. Twenty-six are known to exist.

Dunlap's Declarations were indeed distributed throughout the land, often via riders of horses who may have folded and put them into their saddlebags—which accounts for the folds in some of the existing copies. The words were read aloud to tens of thousands. Abigail Adams told John Adams that in Boston, after the reading in front of the State House, "the [church] bells rang . . . cannon were discharged . . . and every face appeard joyfull."

(above) Rough draft of
the Declaration (1776).
Library of Congress.

(right) A Dunlap broadside
(1776). National Archives.

The Manner in Which the American Colonies Declared Themselves Independant . . . , from *The New, Comprehensive and Complete History of England* by Edward Barnard, London, [1783?]. Library of Congress.

On July 9 Congress ordered that the Declaration be "fairly engrossed [written by hand] on parchment, with the title and stile of 'The unanimous declaration of the thirteen United States of America.'" The person who wrote it out was probably Pennsylvanian Timothy Matlack, who assisted the secretary of the Congress with his duties. Finally, on August 2, according to the journal of the Congress, "the Declaration of Independence being engrossed and compared at the table was signed."

It is this engrossed version that became an American icon. It followed the Congress as it moved about during the Revolution. Along with other government records, it was eventually transferred to the new capital of Washington, D. C. It has remained there ever since, with the exception of trips to Leesburg, Virginia, during the War of 1812, before the British attacked and burned Washington; to Philadelphia for the nation's centennial; and to Fort Knox during World War II.

By 1817, when Congress commissioned the artist John Trumbull to produce four large paintings for the rotunda of the new Capitol, the Declaration had already achieved its near-sacred status, and there was no doubt that one of Trumbull's paintings had to portray the signing of it. Trumbull's twelve-by-eighteen-foot *Declaration of Independence,* completed the next year, became hugely popular. Through public visits to the rotunda and through numerous reproductions, Trumbull's *Declaration* has largely shaped our image of the signing.

The problem is . . . what Trumbull painted wasn't the signing. The moment he portrayed took place neither on July 4, the traditional but wrong date of the signing, nor on August 2, the more likely date for most of the signatures. Rather, Trumbull portrayed the moment when the committee assigned to draft the document—Thomas Jefferson, John Adams, Benjamin Franklin, Robert Livingston, and Roger Sherman—presented their draft to Congress. This took place on June 28.

Trumbull seemed well qualified for the job. He drew maps for the Continental army and later served as a diplomat. In 1786 and then again about a year later, he met with Jefferson in Paris to discuss a Declaration painting, and Trumbull's first sketch of the painting is on the same piece of paper as a sketch Jefferson drew of the room where the delegates met in Philadelphia. After that, Trumbull traveled up and down the east coast

seeking out members of Congress to sketch from life or in some cases collecting portraits of them he could use for a Declaration painting. By 1793 he had already painted a smaller version of what he planned for the Capitol.

Trumbull took his commission for the Capitol very seriously. "I have been constantly occupied on the Declaration of Independance . . . & considering that subject as most interesting to the nation, as well as most decisive of my own reputation," he wrote James Monroe after signing the contract. "The universal interest which my country feels & ever will feel in this event—will in some degree attach to the painting which will preserve the resemblance of forty seven of those patriots to whom we owe this memorable act and all its glorious consequences."

None of this guaranteed the painting's accuracy. Jefferson's memory of the assembly room was faulty, and his sketch got wrong various architectural details.

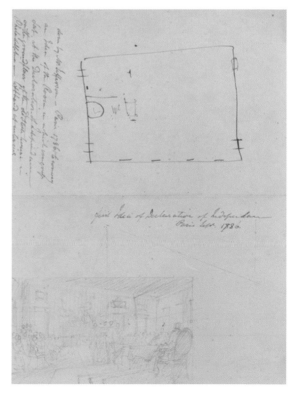

Engrossed Declaration
of Independence (1776).
National Archives.

Trumbull himself later conceded that he "took the liberty of embellishing the background, by suspending upon the wall, military flags and trophies" taken from the enemy. And Trumbull's forty-seven patriots were not an exact match with those present on July 2 or July 4 or those who ultimately signed the Declaration. But this may be unfair to Trumbull. What he wanted, above all, was to capture the solemnity and significance of a moment. In this, he succeeded, and others immediately recognized that. Before delivering the painting to Washington, he took it on a tour of New York, Boston, Philadelphia, and Baltimore. The *New-York Gazette* praised the painting's design and execution as well as its color and perspective and concluded "it is every way worthy of the event which it records."

As for the Declaration itself, the unrolling and rerolling of the parchment took its toll. So, perhaps, did the practice of taking press copies. This process involved placing a damp sheet of paper on a manuscript, pressing it until some of the ink was transferred to the paper, and then transferring the ink onto a copper plate, which could be etched and run on a printing press. As early as 1817, Richard Rush, acting secretary of state, referred to the effects on the document of the "hand of time."

Three years later and fearing these effects, Secretary of State John Quincy Adams commissioned engraver William J. Stone to create an exact copy, which Stone completed in 1823. Stone's prints were considered official copies for government use and were sent to each of the still-living signers: Thomas Jefferson, John Adams, and Charles Carroll of Maryland. It is Stone's image most Americans know, rather than the now largely illegible original. But the original most definitely still exists and is displayed, under armed guard and in a bulletproof case, at the National Archives in Washington, D. C.

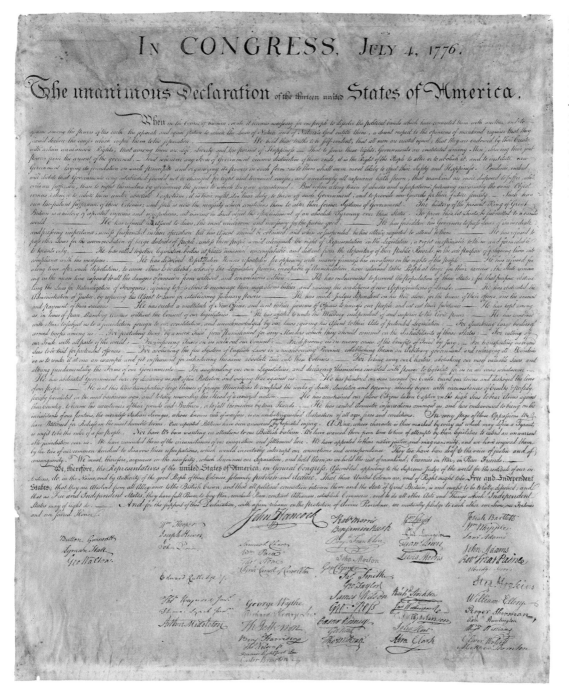

Copy of William Stone's engraving of the Declaration of Independence (1823). Pat and Jerry Epstein American History Document Collection, the Colonial Williamsburg Foundation.

GILBERT STUART, WHOSE PORTRAIT of George Washington appears on the dollar bill, grew up in Rhode Island and moved to Scotland in 1771 when he was sixteen. Stuart's family was loyalist, but that wasn't what led him to leave America. He wanted to study art. Stuart established himself as a successful artist in London and then in Dublin. His daughter Jane, in an 1877 story, wrote, "He was completely absorbed with the idea of returning to America. To execute a portrait of Washington seems to have been his grand purpose."

Jane Stuart was not telling the full story. Stuart returned to America, at least in part, because he was deeply in debt. The artist Charles Robert Leslie recounted the following exchange: "Sir Thomas Lawrence said: 'I knew Stuart well; and I believe the real cause of his leaving *Dollar Bills* England was his having become tired of the inside of some of our prisons.' 'Well, then,' said Lord Holland, 'after all, it was his love of freedom that took him to America.'" Stuart himself admitted that he hoped to "make a fortune by Washington alone" and that, "if I should be fortunate, I will repay my English and Irish creditors."

In 1794 he arrived in Philadelphia, then the U. S. capital, and requested that the president sit for him. The sitting occurred in 1795. Stuart destroyed the first painting but made between twelve and sixteen others. This likeness came to be known as the Vaughan portrait (since one was painted for the Philadelphia merchant John Vaughan, who sent it to his father, Samuel, in London).

Martha Washington was sufficiently impressed by the portrait that she commissioned Stuart to paint a pair of portraits, one of her and one of her husband. George sat for this in 1796 in Germantown, just outside Philadelphia, and the result was the Athenaeum portrait (after the Boston library that later acquired it). It is the Athenaeum that appears on the dollar bill.

A third portrait from life, for which Washington also sat in 1796, became known as the Lansdowne since it was commissioned as a gift for the Marquis of Lansdowne.

The sittings did not go easily. Washington hated to sit for portraits; during a 1772 session with the painter Charles Willson Peale, he admitted

(top left) *Portrait of George Washington* (Vaughan portrait) by Gilbert Stuart (1795–1796). The Colonial Williamsburg Foundation; bequest of Mrs. Edward S. Harkness.

(above) *George Washington* (Lansdowne portrait) by Gilbert Stuart (1796). National Portrait Gallery, Smithsonian Institution; acquired as a gift to the nation through the generosity of the Donald W. Reynolds Foundation.

(left) *George Washington* (Athenaeum portrait) by Gilbert Stuart (1796). William Francis Warden Fund, John H. and Ernestine A. Payne Fund, Commonwealth Cultural Preservation Trust. Jointly owned by the Museum of Fine Arts, Boston, and the National Portrait Gallery, Washington, D.C.

Portrait of George Washington by Charles Willson Peale (1780). The Colonial Williamsburg Foundation; gift of John D. Rockefeller Jr.

he was in "so sullen a mood . . . that I fancy the skill of this gentleman's pencil, will be put to it, in describing to the world what manner of man I am." Stuart was an expert at getting his subjects to talk, which animated their faces and helped him capture their personalities. But Washington, Stuart complained, perked up only when the conversation turned to horses or farming. Moreover, when Washington sat for the Athenaeum and Lansdowne portraits, he had a new set of false teeth that bothered him and distorted the shape of his face.

Though the Athenaeum is the best-known portrait of Washington—indeed, probably the best-known portrait of anyone, ever—Stuart never finished it. Unlike the Vaughan bust and the full-length Lansdowne, the Athenaeum has only Washington's head and shoulders against a partly unfinished background. It's not certain why Stuart never finished the Athenaeum. One theory is that he didn't want to turn it over to Martha Washington and used its unfinished state as reason to hold onto it. That allowed Stuart to use the original to make copies, of which he made more than seventy. These provided a major part of his income for years. Indeed, long before the Athenaeum landed on the dollar bill, Stuart referred to the painting as his "hundred-dollar bill."

How good a likeness of Washington is the Athenaeum? Rembrandt Peale, an artist who admittedly was interested in promoting both his own portraits of Washington and those of his father, Charles Willson Peale, commended "the expression of the countenance" but noted that "the inaccuracy of its drawing and its deviation from the true style and character of [his] head will be evident on a comparison with [Jean-Antoine] Houdon's bust."

Stuart himself ranked the Athenaeum as second only to Houdon's bust, which the French artist sculpted with the aid of a plaster life mask he'd made in 1785.

But Stuart clearly intended the Athenaeum to capture more than Washington's appearance. He wanted to show the man's character. "All his features," an acquaintance recalled Stuart as saying, "were indicative of the strongest and most ungovernable passions." Washington's reputation for "moderation and calmness" was, Stuart recognized, the result of "great self-command." With the nation's future still in doubt, Washington was the one man around whom all could rally, and Stuart's serene Washington provided just the right icon. Stuart's Washington, wrote critic John Neal in an 1823 novel, "was less what Washington was, than what he ought to have been."

The unfinished state of the painting may have added to its iconic stature. "His instinctive rightness of approach," wrote art historian Richard McLanathan, "in showing just the head, without hands, setting, or accessory, is a major reason for its effectiveness. Nothing intrudes to vitiate the extraordinarily controlled power and intensity of the image."

At this point, of course, Stuart's Washington *is* Washington, if only because of the ubiquity of dollar bills. The Athenaeum portrait appeared on numerous private bank notes throughout the first half of the nineteenth century and, as engraved by Alfred Sealey, on federally issued one-dollar notes starting in 1869. Stuart's portrait was also the source for a 1917 engraving by George F. C. Smillie. In Smillie's version, unlike in Sealey's version or Stuart's original, Washington is facing toward the right. Nonetheless, Smillie's version first appeared on the dollar in 1918 and remains there today. As early as 1823, Neal wrote: "If George Washington should appear on earth, just as he sat to Stuart, I am sure that he would be treated as an impostor, when compared with Stuart's likeness of him, unless he produced his credentials."

George Washington by Jean-Antoine Houdon [ca. 1786]. National Portrait Gallery, Smithsonian Institution; gift of Joe L. and Barbara B. Albritton and Robert H. and Clarice Smith and gallery purchase.

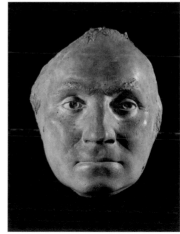

George Washington's Life Mask by Jean-Antoine Houdon (1785). The Pierpont Morgan Library, New York; gift of J. P. Morgan Jr., 1924 AZ151.

Eagles and Turkeys

THE PROCESS THAT PUT THE EAGLE on the Great Seal of the United States—and that made the bird the symbol of America—began on July 4, 1776. Having decided America would be independent, the Continental Congress needed a seal to stamp on its official documents. Congress appointed a committee of John Adams, Benjamin Franklin, and Thomas Jefferson, all three of whom had also served on the committee to draft a declaration of independence. It took a lot longer to agree on an image for the seal than to agree on independence.

Each of the committee members initially proposed an image, none involving an eagle. Adams wanted a scene with Hercules. Jefferson envisioned the children of Israel in the wilderness. Franklin, the committee's chairman, suggested Moses dividing the Red Sea and Pharaoh's army being engulfed in the waters.

Recognizing that they needed help, the committee turned to Pierre Eugène Du Simitière, an artist with some knowledge of heraldry and experience in designing seals. Du Simitière's proposal, which incorporated elements from those of all three committee members, went to Congress in August 1776. Congress promptly tabled the matter.

Congress appointed a second committee in March 1780, which turned to another consultant, Francis Hopkinson. Hopkinson had designed the American flag, and the flag was undoubtedly on his mind when he suggested alternating white and red stripes in the design. But this committee, too, failed to come up with a design that satisfied Congress.

Two years later, Congress appointed a third committee, and this committee appointed William Barton, a lawyer and artist, as its consultant. It was Barton who introduced the eagle—though it was not a bald eagle but a small white eagle with its wings spread. "The eagle displayed," Barton explained, referring to a position in which its wings, body, and legs are displayed, "is the symbol of supreme power and authority and signifies the Congress." Keep in mind that, when Barton wrote this, there was no president; the government of the United States was that of the Articles of Confederation, and the Continental Congress was both the executive and legislative branch.

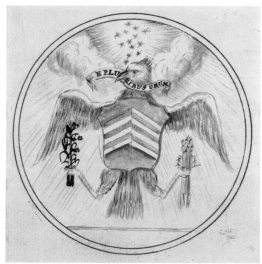

(left) Barton's proposal for the Great Seal (1782). National Archives.

(below) Thomson's proposal for the Great Seal (1782). National Archives.

The committee turned over Barton's work to Charles Thomson, the secretary of Congress. Thomson took ideas from all three committees. From Du Simitière, he took a shield and the motto *E pluribus unum* (out of many, one). From Hopkinson, he took red and white stripes, now on the shield of an eagle, and an olive branch and bundle of arrows, each now in one of the eagle's talons and together symbolizing the nation's love of peace but readiness for war. From Barton's design, Thomson took the eagle, now promoted to a central place in the design and transformed into the native American bald eagle with its wings extending downward as if in flight.

On June 20, 1782, nearly six years after Adams and Franklin and Jefferson began the work, Congress adopted its Great Seal.

(*top*) First die of the Great Seal (1782). National Archives.

(*bottom*) Plate (1805–1815). The Colonial Williamsburg Foundation.

Why did Barton and Thomson (and ultimately Congress) choose an eagle? Undoubtedly, they knew that it was a symbol associated with the Roman Republic, and they were eager to emphasize their own commitment to republicanism. Thomson may also have been familiar with an eighteenth-century edition of Joachim Camerarius's book of third-century emblems chosen from birds and insects, which was used by a 1775 congressional committee charged with designing currency and Continental army "colors," or flags. There is a resemblance between the first emblem in Camerarius's book and the eagle on the Great Seal. In any case, the eagle ended up as a symbol of America adorning everything from porcelain plates to steamboat pilothouses.

Not everyone was pleased with the eagle, especially since the eagle was an aristocratic and military symbol as well as a republican one. Most famously, in a 1784 letter to his daughter, Sarah Bache, Franklin derided the eagle:

> I wish the bald eagle had not been chosen as the representative of our country. He is a bird of bad moral character. He does not get his living honestly. You may have seen him perch'd on some dead tree near the river, where, too lazy to fish for himself, he watches the labour of the fishing hawk; and when that diligent bird has at length taken a fish, and is bearing it to his nest for the support of his mate and young ones, the bald eagle pursues him and takes it from him. With all this injustice, he is never in good case but like those among men who live by sharping and robbing he is generally poor and often very lousy.

The eagle, Franklin continued, "is a rank coward: The little king bird not bigger than a sparrow attacks him boldly and drives him out of the district." In contrast, "the turkey is . . . a much more respectable bird, and withal a true original native of America. . . . He is besides, tho' a little vain and silly, a bird of courage, and would not hesitate to attack a grenadier of the British guards who should presume to invade his farm yard with a red coat on."

Scholars disagree as to whether Franklin was joking. Certainly his style was playful, and historians have noted that Franklin had used the image of an eagle in various works he printed, both before and after it was adopted by Congress.

Historian Lester Olson, however, has argued that Franklin was completely serious. Olson noted that in Franklin's earlier images the eagle represented not the United States but a predatory Great Britain. And his later uses of the image were on publications of official documents, which meant he had no choice in the matter.

If Franklin was serious, he might have been somewhat mollified by the particular image Congress endorsed. "Others object to [it]," he wrote his daughter, "as looking too much like a . . . turkey."

Pilothouse eagle (prob. 1870–1900). The Colonial Williamsburg Foundation; gift of Abby Aldrich Rockefeller.

THE MOST ICONIC IMAGE of patriot musicians is Archibald Willard's *The Spirit of '76*, painted for the 1876 centennial celebrations. "But a glance at it is needed," proclaimed an early promoter of the painting,

to set all the fires of patriotism burning in one's veins, and to compel his footsteps to keep time to the music which he *feels* if he does not hear— for every line in the picture equals a drum tap, and every color thrills like the shrill martial note of the fife. . . .

. . . the trio of homespun musicians are furnishing, with all their might and power, that music which has been since "heard round the world," and whose shrill melody is so full of patriotism that it is, and always will be, the Grand National Tune of America—glorious, grand old Yankee Doodle!

Colonial Williamsburg's fifers and drummers still thrill crowds today as they march through town, but historically their music was only secondarily for the sake of entertainment. Indeed, Shakespeare held the fife in such low esteem that he referred in *The Merchant of Venice* to its "vile squealing" and in *Othello* to its "ear-piercing" tone. During the Revolution, fifes and drums did sometimes boost morale, but this was music played primarily to signal the troops, during both battle and daily life in camp. The fife was shrill enough to be heard over musket fire, the field drum low enough to be heard under cannon fire. It makes perfect sense, therefore, that the act of enlisting or reenlisting was called "following the drum." Drums marked the beginning and end of the Revolution: At Lexington in 1775, a patriot drummer warned the British were coming; at Yorktown in 1781, a British drummer beat a parley and stopped the firing.

What tune the British played at the formal surrender ceremony at Yorktown has been a source of much debate. Tradition holds that it was "The World Turned Upside Down," the words to which went as follows:

If buttercups buzz'd after the bee

If boats were on land, churches on sea

If ponies rode men and if grass ate the cows

And cats should be chased into holes by the mouse

Fifes and Drums

The Spirit of '76 by Archibald M. Willard (1876). Town of Marblehead, Massachusetts.

If the mamas sold their babies
To the gypsies for half a crown
If summer were spring
And the other way 'round
Then all the world would be upside down!

Drum by Henry Fraley (1790–1800). Collection of Colonel J. Craig Nannos.

This was a nice story, fitting the general awareness that the American victory over the world's greatest empire was so unlikely that the world must indeed have turned upside down. The story was told in various forms by such esteemed historians as Henry Commager, Samuel Eliot Morison, and Richard B. Morris. Richard Ketchum, in his history of the Yorktown campaign, described the drums beating to a British march, "a slow, melancholy air, almost certainly 'The World Turn'd Upside Down,' which was a popular tune to which innumerable songs and ballads had been set."

This was almost as good a story as George Washington's cherry tree. And, according to some historians, it was just as untrue. For one thing, the British were hardly in the mood to be playful about their choice of music. As they marched between the French and American victors, many on both sides recalled, the British refused even to look at the Americans. Cornwallis himself avoided the ignominy of surrender by sending his second-in-command, Brigadier General Charles O'Hara. Many of the surrendering redcoats "appeared to be much in liquor," perhaps having emptied their bottles of rum to steel themselves for the ceremony.

Moreover, in all the contemporary accounts—and the surrender was widely reported in newspapers, letters, and journals—there's no mention of "The World Turned Upside Down." The story that the music played was "The World Turned Upside Down" didn't appear in print until 1828, in Alexander Garden's *Anecdotes of the American Revolution*. Garden attributed the story to Major William Jackson, who was secretary to Lieutenant Colonel John Laurens of the Continental army. Laurens was at Yorktown in 1781, but Jackson wasn't there himself, so this account is at best thirdhand.

All of which is not to deny that the surrender at Yorktown turned the world upside down. And for those who insist that such a story be accompanied by music, take heart. Even if the British never played "The World Turned Upside Down," there is at least one reliable report about what the American fifes and drums played. The following description of the surrender comes from the research notes of Jared Sparks, an early nineteenth-century biographer of George Washington who went to France to record firsthand the recollections of the marquis de Lafayette:

> The English marched out between the American and French army drawn up in parallel lines. Lafayette observed as they passed, that they turned their heads towards the French, and would not look at the Americans. A little piqued at this piece of affectation, he thought he would try the effect of music upon them. He ordered his [American] band to strike up Yankee Doodle. The British turned their heads at the sound of this tune.

Fife case (1750–1790). The Colonial Williamsburg Foundation.

Fife (1770–1830). The Colonial Williamsburg Foundation.

BENJAMIN FRANKLIN'S MANY INVENTIONS included a whale oil street lamp whose four-sided design was easier to clean and maintain than the traditional globes; bifocals, or, as Franklin called them, "double spectacles"; the Franklin stove, variations of which are still used today; the armonica, an instrument for which both Mozart and Beethoven composed music; and an odometer to measure the length of post roads (Franklin was deputy postmaster for North America).

Above all, of course, there was the lightning rod, the result of Franklin's realization that metal rods would attract lightning and that through attached wires the electricity might be conducted safely to the ground. In June or July

Kites and Caps

1752 Franklin and his son William famously flew a kite into the clouds. A wire on the kite attracted lightning, and the wet string drew sparks to a wire near the base of the string.

Benjamin West's 1816 painting *Benjamin Franklin Drawing Electricity from the Sky* puts Franklin in the clouds surrounded by angels. West's Franklin is the familiar wise old man, though he was actually only forty-six in 1752.

Franklin was not the first to see a connection between lightning and electricity: Isaac Newton, among others, had already commented on this. Franklin was not even the first to draw sparks from a tall rod since French scientists just north of Paris did so at least a month earlier. But the French acknowledged that they were following a course set by Franklin in his widely published (and translated) writings on electricity. And it was the ever-practical Franklin who turned theory into practice. Just a few months after flying the kite, Franklin's *Poor Richard's Almanack* included instructions for installing lightning rods.

> Provide a small iron rod . . . of such a length, that one end being three or four feet in the moist ground, the other may be six or eight feet above the highest part of the building. To the upper end of the rod fasten about a foot of brass wire, the size of a common knitting-needle, sharpened to a fine point; the rod may be secured to the house by a few small staples. . . . A house thus furnished will not be damaged by lightning, it being attracted by the points, and passing thro the metal into the ground without hurting any thing.

Benjamin Franklin Drawing Electricity from the Sky by Benjamin West (ca. 1816). Philadelphia Museum of Art, Mr. and Mrs. Wharton Sinkler Collection.

Benjamin Franklin, Ne a Boston . . . by Johann Martin Will (1777). The Colonial Williamsburg Foundation.

(left) Ben Franklin Americain by Jean Baptiste Nini (1777). The Colonial Williamsburg Foundation; gift of the Lasser family.

(right) Benjamin Franklin medal by Augustin Dupre (1786). The Colonial Williamsburg Foundation; gift of the Lasser family.

Some religious figures, notably Abbé Jean-Antoine Nollet in France, objected that lightning rods would interfere with the will of God. To which Franklin responded: "Surely the thunder of heaven is no more supernatural than the rain, hail or sunshine of heaven, against the inconveniencies of which we guard by roofs and shades without scruple." Lightning rods soon went up on the Academy of Philadelphia, the Pennsylvania State House, and other buildings throughout the city.

In December 1776, Franklin arrived in Paris to negotiate an alliance between the newly independent United States and France. (By then Franklin was in his seventies and looked like West's wrinkled icon.) He was already famous in France for his experiments with lightning. As his fellow negotiator John Adams resentfully wrote: "His name was familiar to government and people, to kings, courtiers, nobility, clergy, and philosophers, as well as plebeians, to such a degree that there was scarcely a peasant or a citizen, a *valet de chambre,* coachman or footman, a lady's chambermaid or a scullion in a kitchen, who was not familiar with it, and who did not consider him as a friend to human kind."

The French embraced not just Franklin the scientist but also Franklin the American frontiersman. The latter was a strange role in which to cast someone who had rarely ventured into the wilderness. Franklin was the most cosmopolitan of Americans, having spent most of his life in Boston, Philadelphia, and London. Besides, how could he be both a sophisticated scientist and a simple backwoodsman? No matter. Franklin realized, his biographer Walter Isaacson noted, "that the French had read Rousseau, perhaps once too often, and thought of America as a romantic wilderness filled with forest philosophers and natural men."

Franklin reveled in his new role. At Versailles, the most formal and foppish of courts, he wore not a robe and a wig but a frock coat and a marten fur cap. "Figure me," he playfully wrote his friend Emma Thompson, "very plainly dressed, wearing my thin grey straight hair, that peeps out under my only *coiffure,* a fine fur cap; which comes down my forehead almost to my spectacles. Think how this must appear among the powdered heads of Paris!"

The powdered heads loved him for it. Women began wearing their wigs in a style that looked like a fur cap. The French bought snuffboxes, candy boxes, rings, clocks, dishes, and handkerchiefs decorated with his image.

They wore medallions with cameos of Franklin. Just a few weeks after he arrived in France, wrote one commentator, the vogue was "for everyone to have an engraving of M. Franklin over the mantelpiece." Marguerite Gérard's print included as an inscription the words of finance minister Anne-Robert-Jacques Turgot. The Latin translates as "He snatched the lightning from the skies and the scepter from the tyrants."

Franklin himself wrote his daughter in 1779 that the French "have made your father's face as well known as that of the moon." In 1780 he complained that because of the demand for portraits and statues, he "sat so much and so often to painters and statuaries, that I am perfectly sick of it." Among the French artists who portrayed him were Jean-Antoine Houdon and Joseph-Siffred Duplessis. (Duplessis's portrait is perhaps the most familiar image of Franklin today.) King Louis XVI, sick of seeing Franklin's image everywhere, had a porcelain chamber pot made with the American's face at the bottom.

Franklin was as image conscious as any modern celebrity or politician. With remarkable agility, he later recast himself in his autobiography as the embodiment of the American dream, a tradesman who through hard work made himself into a successful businessman. In France, he made the most of his reputation. It gave him access to those in power, and through them he helped secure for America crucial military and financial aid. In February 1778, the French formally agreed to an alliance, which Etienne Pallière commemorated in his painting of that year. Franklin was pictured wearing his fur cap.

Benjamin Franklin by Joseph-Siffred Duplessis (1778). The Metropolitan Museum of Art, New York, Friedsam Collection, Bequest of Michael Friedsam. Image source: Art Resource, NY.

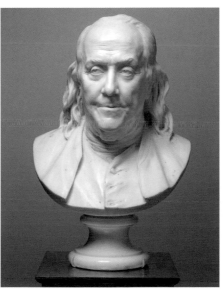

(left) *To the Genius of Franklin* by Marguerite Gérard (1779) after Jean-Honoré Fragonard. Courtesy Davison Art Center, Wesleyan University. Photo by R. J. Phil.

(right) Bust of Benjamin Franklin by Jean-Antoine Houdon (1779). Philadelphia Museum of Art, purchased with funds from the Barra Foundation, the Henry P. McIlhenny Fund in memory of Frances P. McIlhenny, funds bequeathed by Walter E. Stait, the Fiske Kimball Fund, the Women's Committee of the Philadelphia Museum of Art, and donors to the Fund for Franklin. Photo by Graydon Wood.

L ONG BEFORE THE STATUE OF LIBERTY was erected, America personified was a woman. At first, she was most often an Indian queen or princess, a symbol of the entire New World and not just of what would become the United States. Later, she often took on classical features, her feathers sometimes replaced by a helmet or a wreath, her bow and arrows by a spear and shield, her native attire by a toga or robe. Sometimes, especially after the American Revolution, she was called Columbia, her name derived from that of Christopher Columbus. Columbia might dress either as an Indian or a Greek or a Roman goddess or some combination thereof. Often, she was pictured with a liberty cap or liberty pole, both also popular patriotic symbols.

From all these traditions emerged Lady Liberty. She was sometimes known as the Goddess of Liberty, sometimes as just Liberty, and she had many figures and faces. In 1792, she first appeared on coins of the United States. In 1796, she nourished the eagle in Edward Savage's painting *Liberty in the Form of the Goddess of Youth Giving Support to the Bald Eagle.* This painting was much imitated. By the mid-nineteenth century, Lady Liberty had largely displaced her female ancestors. Settlers were pushing Indians off the frontier, and classical and Columbian images conjured up too confusing an array of attributes: wisdom, truth, peace, faith, justice, art, science. These were all very noble but not necessarily or exclusively American. On works of art both fine and popular, Lady Liberty was America.

Lady Liberties

So it was no surprise that, with the centennial of American independence approaching, a young Alsatian sculptor, envisioning a monumental gift from France to the American people, settled on an image of Lady Liberty. The sculptor, Frédéric-Auguste Bartholdi, was a guest at an 1865 dinner party hosted by Édouard-René Lefebvre de Laboulaye, a scholar of American law and history at the Collège de France. At the dinner, Laboulaye proposed that France give America a monument.

(above) *Liberty Crowning Washington* by Catherine Townsend Warner (ca. 1809). The Colonial Williamsburg Foundation; gift of Florence R. Kenyon.

(left) *America* by Justus Danckerts (ca. 1675). The Colonial Williamsburg Foundation.

America by Cornelis Visscher (1650–1660). The Colonial Williamsburg Foundation; gift of the Lasser family.

Liberty by unidentified artist (prob. 1800–1830) after Edward Savage. The Colonial Williamsburg Foundation.

Such a gift made historical sense: Without the support of French troops and leaders, most famously the marquis de Lafayette, America might very well have lost its war for independence. Laboulaye hoped the gift would remind the two nations of their bond. Moreover, he hoped it would encourage democracy in France, at the time ruled by the dictator Napoleon III. The idea gained momentum in 1871 when moderates gained power in France, and Laboulaye stepped up his efforts to raise money from French businesses and citizens.

Bartholdi volunteered to build the statue. The sculptor was drawn to large monuments: In 1856, he toured Egypt and was impressed by the immense Sphinx of Giza. In 1867, he proposed to the Egyptian leader that he erect a monument at the entrance of the Suez Canal, and Bartholdi's drawings for that project—never built—bear some resemblance to those for the Statue of Liberty. Both feature a robed woman holding

Miss Liberty by unidentified artist (prob. 1810–1820). The Colonial Williamsburg Foundation; gift of Abby Aldrich Rockefeller.

up a light. Bartholdi later denied any connection between the two ideas. "At that time my Statue of Liberty did not exist, even in my imagination," he insisted. "How is a sculptor to make a statue which is to serve the purpose of a lighthouse without making it hold the light in the air? Would they have me make the figure . . . hiding the light under its petticoat?"

Bartholdi certainly did not take on the new project merely to reuse some old drawings. Like Laboulaye, Bartholdi was a genuine believer in the cause of liberty. In 1871, the sculptor visited America and in New York Bay came upon Bedloe's Island. He immediately recognized this was the perfect site for his statue. "If I myself felt that spirit here, then it is certainly here that my statue must rise," he wrote Laboulaye, "here where people get their first view of the New World, and where liberty casts her rays on both worlds."

Bartholdi drew on a range of images—classical, European, and American. The statue's face, he later said, was inspired by his own mother's. In 1880, to design a skeleton that would hold up the huge statue, Bartholdi turned to Alexandre-Gustave Eiffel, who less than a decade later would engineer the Eiffel Tower. To actually construct the statue, Bartholdi gathered a team of artisans that met at his workshop in Paris.

Weather vane: *Liberty Enlightening the World* (prob. 1900–1910). The Colonial Williamsburg Foundation; gift of Abby Aldrich Rockefeller.

(right) Bartholdi explaining construction of the hand (ca. 1872). Bettmann/Corbis.

(below) Statue of Liberty in Paris (1887). Bettmann/Corbis.

Joseph Pulitzer's newspaper, *The World,* described the scene: "The workshop was built wholly and solely for the accommodation of this one inmate and her attendants. . . . The Liliputians reached her back hair by means of ladders running from stage to stage of a high scaffolding. . . . A number of pigmies of our species crawling about the inside of what appeared to be a vast caldron used in the sugar-refining trade were understood to be really at work on the crown of her head."

The statue's arrival was delayed while Pulitzer raised money for a pedestal. It made it to New York in 1886—ten years after the centennial it was intended to mark—in 210 wooden crates. (Weighing 225 tons and standing 151 feet tall, the statue was too large to be sent in one piece.)

In June it was installed on its base, and in October it was dedicated by President Grover Cleveland. "We will not forget," proclaimed Cleveland, "that Liberty has here made her home; nor shall her chosen altar be neglected. . . . a stream of light shall pierce the darkness of ignorance and man's oppression, until Liberty enlightens the world."

Throughout the world, replicas abound. Paris has a thirty-six-foot-tall one on an island in the Seine and a nine-foot-tall one in the Jardin du Luxembourg, not far from where Bartholdi once had his home and studio. Las Vegas has a half-size one outside the New York-New York casino; in 2011, the United States Postal Service mistakenly put the Las Vegas statue on its stamp. A plastic and plaster version was erected in Tiananmen Square in Beijing in 1989 during prodemocracy demonstrations. This "Goddess of Democracy," it must be admitted, incorporated some very un-American images. The Beijing students who constructed it started with a model of a young Chinese male athlete and based the head on a woman in a Russian sculpture called "Worker and Collective Farm Woman."

Tiananmen Square (1989). Jacques Langevin/Sygma/Corbis.

It is the Liberty in New York's harbor, of course, that came to hold special meaning for the millions of immigrants who passed it as they arrived in America. It was Emma Lazarus who called the statue "Mother of Exiles" and who in 1883 put these words in her mouth:

"Give me your tired, your poor,
Your huddled masses yearning to breathe free,
The wretched refuse of your teeming shore.
Send these, the homeless, tempest-tost to me,
I lift my lamp beside the golden door!"

Not surprisingly, those opposed to immigration attempted to co-opt the statue, as in one 1890 cartoon whose caption reads: "If you are going to make this island a garbage heap, I am going back to France." But a plaque bearing Lazarus's words was attached to the statue's pedestal in 1903 and remains there today.

The Statue of Liberty (1984). Library of Congress.

"IN YONDER WOODEN STEEPLE," wrote George Lippard in his 1847 story titled "The Fourth of July, 1776," "stands an old man with white hair and sunburnt face. He is clad in humble attire, yet his eye gleams, as it is fixed upon the ponderous outline of the bell, suspended in the steeple there."

The old man cannot read the inscription on the bell, so he calls upon "a flaxen-haired boy, with laughing eyes of summer blue." The boy reads aloud: "Proclaim liberty to all the land and all the inhabitants thereof."

Then the old man sends the child down the steps to await word that the Continental Congress has declared independence. The man anxiously scans the crowd of Philadelphians gathered below until, finally, he spots the boy. The boy's chest swells as he shouts a single word: "Ring!" And so the old man did, and the sound of liberty rang throughout the land.

Liberty Bells

Lippard was fully aware he was writing fiction; his story was one in a collection called *Legends of the American Revolution.* Yet others quickly repeated it as fact, most influentially Benson Lossing in his 1848 book *Seventeen Hundred and Seventy-Six, or the War of Independence.*

There is no evidence that the bell rang on July 4, 1776. Indeed, there's no evidence the Declaration was read to the public until July 8. Even then, though contemporary reports of the reading mention the ringing of bells, none specified the bell in the Pennsylvania State House that later became known as the Liberty Bell. By the late nineteenth century, however, hardly anyone doubted that the Liberty Bell rang for the Declaration of Independence.

As a symbol of American liberty, the State House bell was in one sense a strange choice, since it was originally cast at the Whitechapel Bell Foundry in London. The Pennsylvania Assembly ordered the bell in 1751, well before the Revolution. The inscription on the bell came from Leviticus and was probably meant to honor Pennsylvania's charter. The actual words (which Lippard didn't get quite right) are "Proclaim liberty throughout all the land unto all the inhabitants thereof."

The bell rang for many important events, among them King George III's 1760 ascension to the throne, the 1764 repeal of the Sugar Act, the 1775 Battle of Lexington and Concord, and—just maybe—the July 8, 1776, reading of the Declaration. It rang so often that in 1772 neighbors sent the Assembly a petition complaining that "they are much incommoded and distressed by the too frequent ringing of the great bell in the steeple of the state-house, the inconvenience of which has been often felt severely when some of the petitioners families have been afflicted with sickness, at which times, from its uncommon size and unusual sound, it is extremely dangerous, and may prove fatal."

In 1777, as the British army approached Philadelphia, citizens spirited away the bell, hiding it in the basement of a church in Allentown. The bell returned to Philadelphia the next year and later tolled for, among other events, the ratification of the Constitution and the deaths of George Washington, John Adams, and Thomas Jefferson.

During one of the events for which the bell tolled—exactly which has been the subject of much controversy—the bell cracked. Some reports date the crack to 1824 when it rang for the marquis de Lafayette's visit to Philadelphia. Others blame an 1828 celebration of a British Parliament decision easing discrimination against Catholics. The most common date given for the crack, though with no evidence from contemporary sources, is 1835, when it rang for the death of Chief Justice John Marshall.

According to Emmanuel Rauch, who recalled the events of 1835 in 1911 when he was eighty-six years old, he and several other boys cracked the bell. The boys, including the then-ten-year-old Rauch, had the honor of ringing in Washington's birthday. Rauch told the *New York Times:* "We were working away, and the bell had struck, so far as I can recall, about ten or a dozen times, when we noticed a change in the tone. We kept on ringing . . .

The Bellman Informed of the Passage of the Declaration of Independence, cover of *Graham's Magazine,* June 1854. Library of Congress.

The Liberty Bell in the Liberty Bell Center. Courtesy Independence National Historical Park.

but, after a while, the steeplekeeper noticed the difference, too. Surmising that something might be wrong, he told us to stop pulling the rope." The steeple keeper then told the boys to go home, which they did.

Most likely, the bell's problems dated back to well before Rauch and his friends were born. In 1753, after the bell was first hung in the State House, Isaac Norris, who had signed the Assembly's letter ordering the bell, noted: "I had the mortification to hear that it was cracked by the stroke of the clapper without any other viollence as it was hung up to try the sound." Two Philadelphia foundry workers twice melted down and recast the bell, but Norris was still displeased with the results.

The two recastings probably weakened the bell, making it susceptible to cracks. In any case, in 1846 the crack expanded to an extent that it ruined the bell's sound and led its keepers to fear it would fracture further. Recorded the Philadelphia *Public Ledger* of February 26: "*The old Independence Bell. . . . rang its last clear note on Monday last, in honor of the birth day of Washington, and now hangs in the great city steeple irreparably cracked and forever dumb.*"

More than one hundred fifty years later, London's Whitechapel Bell Foundry is still defending its craftsmanship. Whitechapel's website notes that, if a bell is struck and not allowed to ring freely, because either the clapper or some part of the frame or fittings are in contact with the bell, then a crack can easily develop. The website also recounts that during the American bicentennial some mock protesters marched outside the foundry with signs proclaiming "We Got a Lemon" and "What about the Warranty?" The company responded that it would be happy to replace the bell—as long as it was returned in its original packaging.

Back in the nineteenth century, the crack was not entirely inappropriate for a symbol of liberty in a land that still allowed slavery, and abolitionists adopted it as their own symbol. The first documented use of the name "Liberty Bell" came in the 1835 edition of the American Anti-Slavery Society's *Anti-Slavery Record*. (Before then, it was usually called the "State House bell.") In Boston, William Lloyd Garrison's abolitionist newspaper, *The Liberator,* published a poem titled "The Liberty Bell" in 1839. Another group of Boston abolitionists titled their publication *The Liberty Bell* and often featured poems about and illustrations of the bell.

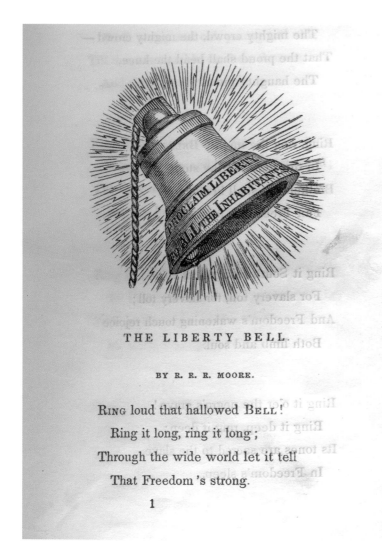

THE LIBERTY BELL.

BY R. R. R. MOORE.

RING loud that hallowed BELL!
Ring it long, ring it long;
Through the wide world let it tell
That Freedom's strong.

1

First page of "The Liberty Bell," from *The Liberty Bell,* published by the Massachusetts Anti-Slavery Fair, Boston, 1844. Courtesy Independence National Historical Park.

Later, women's suffragists used the Liberty Bell, sending around the country a full-size replica. They did not ring their bell until 1920 when women won the right to vote.

This being America, the Liberty Bell also has been used to promote products and services. It has appeared in ads for, among others, banks, foods, stores, and railroads. "The Liberty Bell sounded freedom from a foe," proclaimed a 1915 ad for flour in a Salt Lake City newspaper. "The women of this region have been freed from the worries of poor bread by White Fawn Flour." In 1996, in full-page ads in newspapers throughout the country, Taco Bell announced it had purchased the bell and renamed it the "Taco Liberty Bell." This went a bit far for outraged Americans, and the company quickly issued a press release explaining that the ads were an April Fools' Day joke.

More seriously contentious were the plans, begun in the 1990s, for a new home for the bell in a pavilion to be built a block from Independence Hall. Should the bell be treated primarily as a symbol of the liberty achieved in 1776? Or should more emphasis be placed on the bell's role as an inspiration for those, in particular African Americans, whose liberty was denied? Even the site raised issues. Here had stood a mansion in which George Washington had lived when Philadelphia was the nation's capital—and with Washington had come enslaved African Americans from Mount Vernon. The new Liberty Bell Center, opened in 2003, showcases the bell's role in the abolitionist, women's suffrage, and civil rights movements. Concluded historian Gary Nash: "Now it is truly everyone's bell."

Liberty Bell for Suffrage
(1916). Library of
Congress.

THOUGH LARGELY FORGOTTEN today, to the American patriots of the eighteenth century, liberty trees and liberty poles were symbols of their cause at least as prominent as liberty bells or lady liberties. This made sense: In a continent covered by forests, trees offered colonists shelter and warmth and the promise of a new start. Trees might also have reminded Revolutionaries of stories of earlier rebels: Think Robin Hood in Sherwood Forest. And many Connecticut patriots could recite the legend of the Charter Oak, a tree in Hartford where in 1687 colonists had allegedly hidden their charter to prevent the king's agents from seizing it.

It was in Boston, however, that the liberty tree took root. Specifically, it was at the intersection of Essex and Newbury Streets. Here stood a large elm tree known—until 1765—as the Great Elm or the Great Tree. On August

Liberty Trees

14 of that year, Bostonians woke to find hanging from one of its branches an effigy of Andrew Oliver, whose job was to distribute the stamps authorized by the much-despised Stamp Act. That evening, a crowd led by shoemaker Ebenezer Mackintosh paraded the dummy though the streets of Boston and set it afire near Oliver's house. The next day, Oliver sent word through friends of his resignation.

On September 11, news reached Boston that in London William Pitt, a Stamp Act opponent, was to become prime minister. Quickly, a large copper plate was affixed to the tree's trunk. On the plate were the words "The Tree of Liberty."

Over the next decade, Boston's Liberty Tree was the site of numerous patriot demonstrations. In November 1765, crowds hung in effigy a supporter of the Stamp Act. Paul Revere's engraving pictures him on the tree while a dragon, symbolizing the Stamp Act, threatens the Magna Charta. In May 1766, when news reached Boston that the Stamp Act had been repealed, the *Boston-Gazette* reported the tree was "decorated in a splendid manner." In January 1774, a crowd enraged by Parliament's Tea Act tarred and feathered a British customs official. Philip Dawe's print of the scene shows in the background both the Boston Tea Party and the Liberty Tree, which in this case has become a gallows. Johann Martin Will's print, also published soon after the Boston Tea Party, symbolizes the British closing of Boston's port by placing Bostonians in a cage hanging from the Liberty Tree.

(above) *A View of the Year 1765* by Paul Revere (1765). Courtesy American Antiquarian Society.

(left) *The Bostonian's Paying the Excise-Man, or Tarring & Feathering*, attributed to Philip Dawe (1774). The Colonial Williamsburg Foundation.

(right) *The Bostonians in Distress* by Johann Martin Will (1774). The Colonial Williamsburg Foundation.

James Pike's powder horn (1776). Chicago History Museum.

In 1775, the British army occupied Boston, and loyalists seized the opportunity to chop down the tree. By then, though, the tree's seeds had spread beyond Boston. John Dickinson honored it in his 1768 "Liberty Song" and Thomas Paine in his 1775 poem "Liberty Tree," which reads in part:

> From the east to the west, blow the trumpet to arms,
> Thro' the land let the sound of it flee,
> Let the far and the near,—all unite with a cheer,
> In defence of our *Liberty tree*.

During the war, many New England soldiers carved liberty trees on their powder horns. James Pike's powder horn depicts not only the tree but the Battle of Lexington, with the British soldiers labeled "Regulars, the Aggressors" and the patriots "Provincials Defending."

Outside of New England, liberty poles often played the part of liberty trees. In New York City, patriots erected a liberty pole near the common to celebrate the repeal of the Stamp Act. British soldiers repeatedly cut it down, often leading to skirmishes. The pole provided New Yorkers with an advantage their fellow patriots in New England lacked: Unlike trees, new poles could quickly replace old ones. New York's patriots also learned to protect their pole with iron, as can be seen in Pierre Eugène Du Simitière's drawing *Raising of the Liberty Pole in New York City*. Liberty poles were often topped by liberty caps, a symbol of emancipation of slaves dating back to Roman times.

In 1787, Thomas Jefferson wrote, metaphorically but surely with an awareness of the tree's history, that "the tree of liberty must be refreshed from time to time with the blood of patriots and tyrants." At the time, Jefferson was in France, where the liberty tree became one of the main icons of the French Revolution. Back in America, poles cropped up in Pennsylvania during the Whiskey Rebellion in 1794 when farmers protested a federal tax; after the passage of the 1798 Sedition Act, which authorized fines and prison for those who defamed the government; and as campaign symbols during the 1820s. (Andrew Jackson, whose nickname was Old Hickory, favored poles of hickory; Henry Clay of Ashland, Kentucky, used ash poles.)

As a campaign symbol, liberty poles—and trees—had already lost much of their iconic power. Why did these icons fade away while others like liberty bells or lady liberties endured? At least for the trees, one reason is that those that weren't cut down eventually died. Historian Alfred Young has argued that it wasn't just the British but also American conservatives who, at least metaphorically, chopped down the trees. Liberty trees and poles were often gathering points for radicals. The skirmishes that took place around them were often led by working-class artisans like shoemaker Ebenezer Mackintosh, hardly one of our best-known founding fathers, and the trees and poles were embraced as symbols less by generals than by soldiers like the farmer and militiaman James Pike. That liberty poles became prominent symbols of the French Revolution also scared American conservatives. Whatever the reasons, by the mid-nineteenth century, the trees and poles were largely gone from America's memory.

Raising of the Liberty Pole in New York City by Pierre Eugène Du Simitière (ca. 1770). The Library Company of Philadelphia.

P AUL REVERE'S FAMOUS ENGRAVING, perhaps the most famous
illustration of the Revolutionary period, leaves little doubt about who
was to blame for what Revere called "the bloody massacre perpetrated in
King Street." The illustration shows British soldiers in a line, firing point-
blank at a crowd of unarmed townspeople, apparently at the order of their
captain, Thomas Preston. In reality, the origins of the Boston Massacre are
much murkier—and so are the origins of Revere's illustration, which the
famed silversmith may very well have copied from another artist's work.

First, the Massacre. Soldiers did indeed shoot Bostonians on that
evening of March 5, 1770, killing three on the spot and mortally wounding
two others. To patriots like Revere and Samuel Adams, the violence was
the direct and inevitable result of British oppression, in particular that of
the British soldiers who were in Boston to enforce unpopular
trade regulations. The victims were the first heroes of the
Revolution to come. Until 1784, many Americans celebrated
their independence on March 5 rather than July 4.

Massacres

Not surprisingly, the British had a different view of the
events. Some London newspapers suggested the Bostonians were after the
king's coffers in the customhouse. Others accused patriot leaders of planning
the incident, perhaps even with the hope of turning its victims into martyrs.
To loyalists, this was not the Boston Massacre but "an unhappy disturbance."
A mid-nineteenth-century illustration by Alonzo Chappel presents the
deaths as the result of a chaotic mob scene rather than anything planned by
either the soldiers or the patriots. In Chappel's illustration, the soldiers are
disorganized, Preston appears to be signaling for them to stop firing, and
some of the Bostonians are carrying clubs and clearly threatening.

The evidence presented at the soldiers' trials seems closer to Chappel's
version than Revere's. The defense attorney, none other than future president
John Adams, argued that the soldiers acted in self-defense. One defense
witness was Dr. John Jeffries, a friend of Samuel Adams, who had treated
Patrick Carr, one of the victims. Jeffries testified that Carr, as he lay dying,
told him he'd heard many voices cry out to kill the soldiers. Carr added
"that he did not blame the man whoever he was, that shot him." The jury
acquitted Preston and six of the soldiers of murder and found two other
soldiers guilty of the lesser charge of manslaughter.

The Bloody Massacre Perpetrated in King Street . . . by Paul Revere (1770). The Colonial Williamsburg Foundation.

(right) *Boston Massacre,* engraving by an unidentified artist after Alonzo Chappel. National Archives.

(below) Sketch of Boston Massacre by Paul Revere (1770). Boston Public Library.

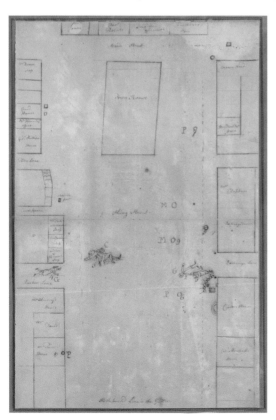

Historians continue to debate the verdicts, but there's no doubt that in making his engraving Revere was more interested in the propaganda value of a massacre than in accurately portraying the details. The "Butcher's Hall" sign on a coffeehouse popular with British officers was clearly meant as a barb. The casualty list at the bottom of the illustration is inaccurate, identifying as mortally wounded two who survived. The illustration seems to have entirely omitted Crispus Attucks, one of the victims and an escaped slave who was the son of an African father and Native American mother. If Attucks is in the picture at all, he has been turned into a white man. Revere himself presented a more accurate view of the event in a pen-and-ink diagram plan of King Street. He may have prepared this for use at the soldiers' trials, though it does not appear to have been used in court.

As for the famous engraving's origins, Revere may have copied it from the Boston painter and engraver Henry Pelham. The image generally attributed to Pelham is certainly very similar to the one generally attributed to Revere. The most noticeable differences are the headings and, in Revere's, the addition of the entirely fictional "Butcher's Hall" sign.

On March 29, 1770, Pelham wrote to Revere accusing him of copying the work. "I thought I had entrusted it in the hands of a person who had more regard to the dictates of honour and justice than to take the undue advantage you have done of the confidence and trust I reposed in you. But I find I was mistaken," Pelham angrily wrote. It was as bad as if, Pelham added, "you had plundered me on the highway." A week later, Pelham advertised his print in Boston newspapers, describing it as "an original print . . . taken from the spot."

There's no record of Revere responding to Pelham. In Revere's defense, it was common at the time for engravers to take designs wherever they found them without the original artist's permission. In any case, Revere must have somehow mollified Pelham. Four years later, in 1774, Revere was doing engraving work for Pelham.

Fruits of Arbitrary Power, or the Bloody Massacre by Henry Pelham (1770). Courtesy American Antiquarian Society.

ON THE FRONT OF THE DOLLAR BILL is the familiar portrait of George Washington. On the back on the right side is the almost-as-familiar picture of the American eagle. It's the left side of the back of the bill that's perplexing, even a bit spooky: a pyramid topped by a triangle with an eye inside it and light radiating from it.

Like the eagle, the pyramid and eye come from the Great Seal of the United States, which has been used to stamp official documents since Congress adopted it in 1782. Yet the pyramid and eye are such strange images—so seemingly un-American—that many have suspected they were the result of a conspiracy involving Freemasons. Originally a medieval guild for stonemasons, the Masons had, by the time of the Revolution, evolved in both England and America into a semisecret society. The pyramid and the eye were both Masonic symbols.

Pyramids and Eyes

Many of the founding fathers were Masons, among them Benjamin Franklin, John Hancock, James Madison, James Monroe, John Paul Jones, Paul Revere, and George Washington. Many members of the Sons of Liberty, a secret society whose aims were explicitly Revolutionary, were Masons. Indeed, in the seventeenth and eighteenth centuries, many suspected that Masons were behind not only the Great Seal but also the Revolution.

The connections between the Republic and Freemasonry were on public display in 1793 when Washington, accompanied by fellow Masons, led a procession to the site of the Capitol to lay the building's cornerstone. By this time, the Masons had little connection to their origins of actually laying stones; the physical cornerstone was a symbol of the Masonic principles of liberty and virtue on which the Republic was to be built. The president wore Masonic regalia, and the ceremony included a blessing of the stone with Masonic symbols. On the cornerstone Washington placed a silver plate that stated the date: "the 18th day of September, 1793, in the eighteenth year of American independence . . . and in the year of Masonry, 5793."

Yet the actual influence of Masons on the Revolution has been much exaggerated. While the secrecy of the society makes numbers hard to verify, only nine of fifty-five men who signed the Declaration were definitely Masons, and only thirteen of the thirty-nine who signed the Constitution.

A version of the reverse
of the Great Seal by
James Trenchard [1786].
Library of Congress.

ANNUIT CŒPTIS:

M.DCC.LXXVI.

NOVUS ORDO SECLORUM.

(*above*) Barton's proposal for the reverse of the Great Seal (1782). National Archives.

(*right*) Fifty-dollar bill by Francis Hopkinson (1778). Courtesy American Antiquarian Society.

And the ranks of Freemasons also included plenty of loyalists, among them Benedict Arnold. Wrote Franklin of the Masons: "They are in general a very harmless sort of people; and have no principles or practices that are inconsistent with religion and good manners."

How, then, to account for the appearance of Masonic symbols on the Great Seal and later the dollar bill?

The eye, known as the eye of Providence, can be traced to an August 1776 sketch for the seal prepared by Eugène Du Simitière, a consultant brought in by a congressional committee consisting of John Adams, Benjamin Franklin, and Thomas Jefferson. Congress tabled Du Simitière's proposal, but the eye reappeared in the 1782 proposal by another consultant, William Barton.

A thirteen-step pyramid appeared on fifty-dollar bills issued by Congress in 1778 and designed by Francis Hopkinson. Barton's design for the seal—almost certainly influenced by Hopkinson's currency—also included the thirteen-step pyramid.

It was Charles Thomson, secretary of Congress, who later that year combined elements of Du Simitière's and Barton's designs. Thomson added the mottos *Annuit coeptis* (he [God] has favored our undertakings) over the eye and *Novus ordo seclorum* (a new order of the ages) beneath the pyramid.

Thomson's remarks to the Continental Congress spelled out what the images meant:

> The pyramid signifies strength and duration. The eye over it and the motto allude to the many signal interpositions of Providence in favour of the American cause. The date underneath is that of the Declaration of Independence, and the words under it signify the beginning of the new American era, which commences from that date.

Note that Thomson was definitely not a Mason. Nor were Adams or Jefferson or Du Simitière or Barton.

The pyramid and the eye were undeniably Masonic symbols, but it's highly unlikely the designers—or Congress—chose them for that reason. The pyramid and the eye were not just Masonic symbols. Many non-Masonic artists have used an eye to symbolize an all-seeing God, and many non-Masons in the eighteenth century were fascinated by Egypt. Both Hopkinson and Barton might have seen *Pyramidographia* in the Library Company of Philadelphia. This book included a drawing with a pyramid very similar to Hopkinson's. "It seems likely," wrote Richard Patterson and Richardson Dougall in their exhaustive history of the Great Seal, "that the designers . . . and the Masons took their symbols from parallel sources."

Getting the pyramid and eye from the seal to the bill took more than 150 years and had less to do with the image than the motto underneath it: *Novus ordo seclorum.* Since "a new order of the ages" sounded a lot like a "New Deal," it appealed to President Franklin Roosevelt. Roosevelt's secretary of agriculture, Henry Wallace, later took credit for the idea.

> In 1934 . . . I was waiting in the outer office of Secretary [of State Cordell] Hull and as I waited I amused myself by picking up a State Department publication which was on a stand there entitled, "The History of the Seal of the United States." Turning to page 53 I noted the colored reproduction of the reverse side of the [Great] Seal. The Latin phrase Novus ordo seclorum impressed me as meaning the New Deal of the Ages. Therefore I took the publication to President Roosevelt and suggested a coin be put out with the obverse and reverse sides of the Seal. . . . [Roosevelt] suggested that the Seal be put out on the dollar bill rather than a coin and took the matter up with the secretary of the Treasury.

Snakes

IN 1754, WITH THE FRENCH AND INDIANS attacking British settlements in the Ohio Valley, Benjamin Franklin proposed "a plan for the union of all the colonies." To illustrate the need for unity, Franklin published (and some think drew) one of America's earliest political cartoons and perhaps the earliest symbol of a united America (albeit under British rule). The picture, which appeared in the May 9 *Pennsylvania Gazette,* was a severed snake representing the disunited colonies. The caption read: "Join, or Die." Franklin may have taken the idea from a seventeenth-century French image of a snake cut in two.

The plan for unity came to naught. The colonies feared each other as much as any external threat, whether French or Indian. Two decades later, though, the colonies were more united and the threat was now clearly the British. Snakes representing the united colonies appeared on the mastheads of the *New-York Journal,* the *Massachusetts Spy,* and the *Pennsylvania Journal,* in the case of the *New-York Journal* replacing the royal insignia, the king's arms. Lest anyone mistake the meaning of the *New-York Journal*'s change, on January 19, 1775, a rival newspaper, *Rivington's New-York Gazetteer,* presented this explanation:

'Tis true, that the arms of a good *British king,*
Have been forc'd to give way to a snake—with a sting;
Which some would interpret, as tho' it imply'd,
That the king by a wound of that serpent had died.

The *Massachusetts Spy* depicted a segmented snake, engraved by Paul Revere, battling a dragon. Publisher Isaiah Thomas spelled it out: "The dragon represented Greatbritain, and the snake the colonies."

As the colonies became more united, the snakes became less segmented. After the first Continental Congress convened, the *New-York Journal* replaced its disjointed snake with a united one and inscribed on its body: "United now alive and free." An officer's button purportedly found near a 1778 battlefield in Monmouth, New Jersey, displayed a rattlesnake encircling thirteen stars. In British illustrations, too, snakes became popular symbols of America. A 1782 etching attributed to James Gillray shows the American snake coiled into three sections, two encircling British forces that had surrendered and a third advertising "An apartment to lett for military gentlemen."

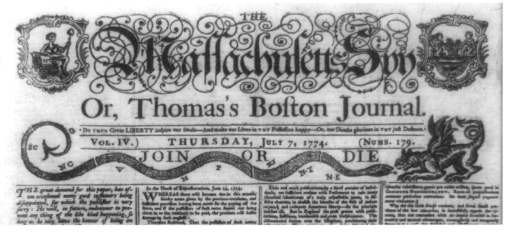

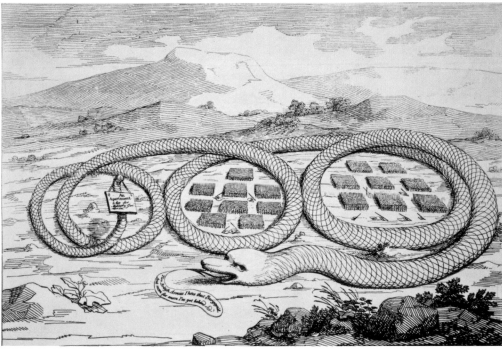

(top left) *Join, or Die* by Benjamin Franklin, *Pennsylvania Gazette* (1754). Library of Congress.

(top right) American officer's "Rattlesnake & Stars" button (ca. 1778). The Colonial Williamsburg Foundation.

(left) *Join or Die* by Paul Revere, *Massachusetts Spy* (1774). Library of Congress.

(bottom) *The American Rattle Snake*, attributed to James Gillray (1782). The Colonial Williamsburg Foundation.

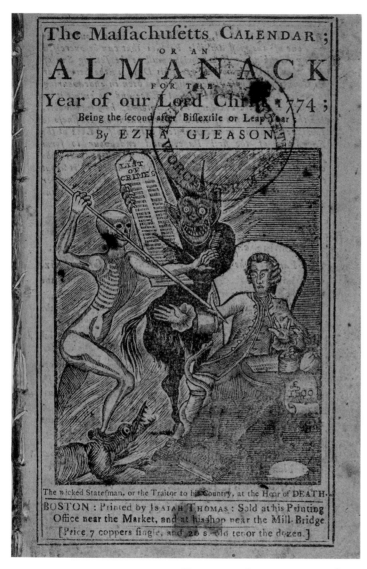

The Wicked Statesman, or the Traitor to His Country at the Hour of Death, cover of Massachusetts Calendar; or an Almanack for the Year of Our Lord Christ 1774... by Ezra Gleason, Boston, 1774. Courtesy American Antiquarian Society.

Rattlesnakes became especially popular, appearing on various state flags as well as navy and army flags and often coiled and ready to strike. Below the snake were often the words "Don't tread on me." The phrase has sometimes been attributed to Franklin, probably because of his role in promulgating the "Join, or Die" snake, but most historians credit them to Christopher Gadsden, a leading South Carolina patriot and a member of the Continental Congress. At the very least, Gadsden must have liked the image, since in February 1776 he presented a flag with it to the South Carolina provincial Congress. In the late twentieth and early twenty-first centuries, what came to be known as the Gadsden flag was adopted by libertarians and then Tea Party activists.

In one sense, the snake was a strange choice for Americans. "To those familiar with the Judeo-Christian tradition," wrote historian Lester Olson, "the image of the snake ought to have had connotations of wickedness, yet here was a predominantly Christian culture that seemed to welcome the image as a representation of themselves."

Even as Americans embraced the snake image, snakes continued to connote wickedness. In 1774, the snake not only appeared on the Massachusetts Spy's masthead but also on the cover of an almanac, also published by Thomas. On the almanac the snake is wrapped around Governor Thomas Hutchinson's leg and is a symbol of evil. The Spy went so far as to explicitly deny that the snake on its masthead had anything to do with the one in the Garden of Eden, explaining in its September 15, 1774, issue that "the snake ye with wonder behold, / Is not the deceiver so famous of old."

Why, then, use the snake at all? Partly it may have been because its long and winding shape seemed similar to that of the colonies—and later the states—along the coast of North America. In 1775, a *Pennsylvania Journal* writer noted that the rattlesnake, like America, "never begins an attack, nor, when once engaged, ever surrenders." Best of all, said the *Journal* writer, "the Rattle-Snake is found in no other quarter of the world besides America."

Eventually, though, snakes simply wouldn't do. After the Revolution, they were used less and less frequently as a symbol of America, and, when they were used, it was often alongside the increasingly ascendant eagle. Indeed, the snake was sometimes again a symbol of treachery. Around 1800, for example, an anti-Jefferson print portrayed the eagle protecting the Constitution while Jefferson tried to burn it on the "Altar of Gallic Despotism." A snake was firmly wrapped around the altar.

The Providential Detection (ca. 1800). The Library Company of Philadelphia.

THE PROVIDENTIAL DETECTION

I T TAKES A BIT MORE THAN the dawn's early light to make out the origins of the flag. But it can be done.

Let's start with the stripes. In 1769 some Bostonians raised a flag of alternating red and white stripes to celebrate the recall of their unpopular British governor, Francis Bernard. In 1773 Boston's Sons of Liberty flew a flag with nine red and white stripes representing the nine colonies that had attended the Stamp Act Congress. In 1775 the Philadelphia Light Horse included thirteen silver stripes in the upper left corner of its flag. In January 1776 at the Continental army's camp near Boston, George Washington ordered raised a flag known as the Continental Colors. It had thirteen stripes, alternating between red and white and representing the thirteen colonies.

These various flags may have been inspired by that of the British East India Company, which from 1707 flew a flag of red and white stripes. This seems a strange source: Why choose an image associated with the country whose policies you were protesting? But well into the 1770s all but the most disgruntled colonists hoped they might resolve their differences with the mother country. Even when Washington raised the Continental Colors, the Declaration of Independence was still six months in the future. Indeed, the Continental Colors featured not just red and white stripes but also, in the corner where we are used to seeing white stars in a field of blue, the Union Jack—the British flag created in 1606 by King James I. American forces flew the Continental Colors in 1776 and 1777, primarily at sea but also at some forts.

Still, Washington recognized the problem of a Union Jack in the American flag. A few days after the Continental Colors was raised near Boston, he noted in a letter to his military secretary that the British there thought the flag was "a signal of submission." Washington added that "by this time I presume they begin to think it strange that we have not made a formal surrender." The Continental Congress also saw the need for a change. On June 14, 1777, Congress resolved "that the flag of the . . . United States be thirteen stripes, alternate red and white: that the union be thirteen stars, white in a blue field, representing a new constellation."

Stars and Stripes

(*left*) Flag of the Philadelphia Light Horse, now the First Troop Philadelphia City Cavalry (ca. 1775). Photo by John Bansemer 2011.

(*below left*) The Union Jack (modern reproduction). The Colonial Williamsburg Foundation.

(*below right*) The Continental Colors (modern reproduction). The Colonial Williamsburg Foundation.

The Continental Colors must have influenced the stripes. We do not know why Congress chose stars, though they were common in Masonic and other imagery and Washington may have used them as his army's flag as early as 1776.

The task of translating Congress's rather vague instructions into a specific design most likely fell to Francis Hopkinson, a signer of the Declaration of Independence and still a congressman from New Jersey. Hopkinson was also a poet, essayist, inventor, musician, and artist. Three years later, Hopkinson wrote a letter to the Continental Board of Admiralty noting the government had adopted a number of his designs, including several "devices for the Continental currency" and "the flag of the United States of America." Hopkinson suggested that "a quarter cask of the public wine" would "be a proper and reasonable reward for these labours of fancy." Hopkinson also sent a bill for "sundry devices drawings mottos etc." The first item on it was "the great naval flag of the United States."

Hopkinson charged nine pounds for his design of the flag. He was never paid. The Board of Treasury rejected his bill on the grounds that he "was not the only person consulted on those exhibitions of fancy" and that he was already receiving a salary from Congress. But note: The board did not at any point deny Hopkinson's claim to have designed the flag.

In any case, the particular design was not then considered a matter of great import. Early flags were made by hand and exhibited many variations. Sometimes the stars were arranged in a circle, sometimes in rows or a straight line. Sometimes the stars had four points, sometimes five or six or eight. Sometimes the flags included other emblems, such as an eagle, and sometimes words. Sometimes dots replaced stars. And military units throughout the new United States continued to fly their own regimental flags more often than the Stars and Stripes.

It was not until the Civil War that the flag became the primary symbol of American patriotism. The "Star-Spangled Banner" was played at rallies throughout the North, and "The Battle Cry of Freedom" (which begins with "Yes, we'll rally round the flag, boys") was also popular. It wasn't until the end of the nineteenth century that students began to recite the Pledge of Allegiance in public schools.

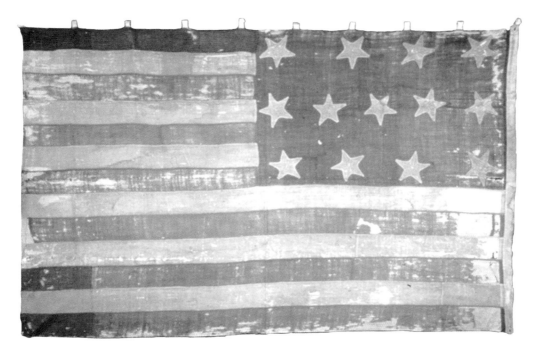

National 13-star flag ("Jonathan Fowle" or "Castle William" flag) (ca. 1781). Courtesy Commonwealth of Massachusetts, Art Commission.

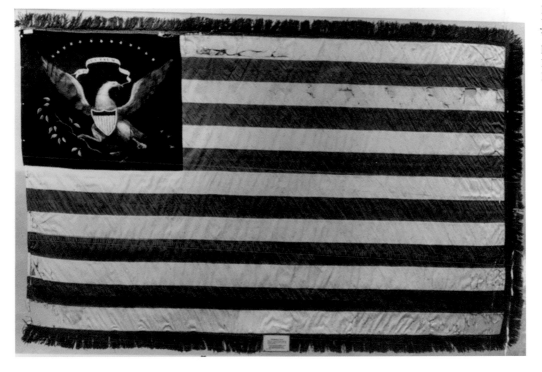

Flag of General Philip John Schuyler of New York (prob. 1784 or later). Independence National Historical Park.

The flag continued to change, adding stars for each new state. In 1958, the year before Alaska and Hawaii became states, a seventeen-year-old high school student in Lancaster, Ohio, designed the fifty-star flag as part of a history assignment. Robert Heft received a B minus because his teacher (like most professional flag makers) assumed Alaska but not Hawaii would become a state. Heft ultimately got more out of the flag than Hopkinson: When Congress accepted his design, the teacher upped the grade to an A.

Of course, neither Heft nor Hopkinson ever approached the fame of a Philadelphia seamstress named Elizabeth Griscom Ross. The story of Betsy Ross came to the fore in 1870 when her grandson William Canby read a paper on the history of the flag to the Historical Society of Philadelphia. According to Canby, in a letter to George Henry Preble, he was eleven years old when his grandmother told him and other family members how she came to create the first flag:

> Washington was a frequent visitor at my grandmother's house *before* receiving his command of the army. She embroidered his shirt ruffles, and did many other things for him. He knew her skill with the needle. Col. Ross [Betsy Ross's late husband's uncle George Ross] with . . . Robt. Morris, and Gen. Washington called upon Mrs. Ross, and told her they were a committee of Congress, and wanted her to make the flag from the drawing, a rough one, which upon her suggestions was redrawn by General Washington in pencil in her back-parlor. This was prior to the Declaration of Independence; and I fix the date to be during Washington's visit to Congress from New York in June, 1776, when he came, to confer upon the affairs of the army, the flag being no doubt one of these affairs.

There is no doubt that Betsy Ross made flags. It is even conceivable that she knew Washington, if we are to believe the testimony of Canby and other family members. Ross biographer Marla R. Miller argued in her 2010 book that this experienced upholsterer was much more likely than the lawyer Hopkinson or the planter Washington to recognize, as her family attested, how much easier it would be to produce a lot of stars with five points rather than the six Washington supposedly envisioned.

Still, there is no evidence that prior to its resolution of June 1777 Congress discussed, let alone turned to anyone to sew, a new national flag. It requires a great deal of speculation to jump from the evidence that Ross produced American flags to the conclusion that, as Canby claimed, her suggestions led Washington to redraw the design "in her back-parlor."

Why, then, do we remember Betsy Ross? Perhaps America needed a founding mother to go with the founding fathers. It is a comfortably domestic story: George and Betsy get together to conceive a flag—and a nation. Wrote historian Marc Leepson:

> The Betsy Ross story served as a sort of counterbalance to the message promulgated by organizations such as Elizabeth Cady Stanton and Susan B. Anthony's all-female National Woman Suffrage Association [founded in 1869, the year before Canby presented his grandmother's story]. . . . The picture presented of Betsy Ross —doing a traditional woman's job of sewing at home . . . contained the opposite message presented by the women who were outspokenly bold as they worked for the vote.

But, even if the Betsy Ross story initially spread in part as backlash to the suffrage movement, it is also possible to see Ross as a feminist heroine. Leepson admits as much, describing her as "a strong-willed woman, twice widowed, running her own successful business out of her home while caring for her children." And, even if Ross did not remove one of the points in the flag's stars, as Miller speculated, and even if she had no role at all in the flag's design, Ross deserves credit for having sewn many a flag. It's difficult to argue with Miller's broader point that the Revolution's success "hinged not just on eloquent political rhetoric or character displayed in combat, but also on Betsy Ross and thousands of people just like her—women and men who went to work every day and took pride in a job well done."

Uncle Sams

T HE MOST COMMON THOUGH not entirely convincing story about Uncle Sam's origins traces him back to Samuel Wilson, a Troy, New York, meatpacker who supplied beef and pork to the American army during the War of 1812. Here is a version of the story that appeared in 1832:

Immediately after the declaration of the last war with England, Elbert Anderson, of New York, then a contractor, visited Troy, on the Hudson, where was concentrated, and where he purchased, a large quantity of provisions—beef, pork, etc. The inspectors of these articles at that place, were Messrs. Ebenezer and Samuel Wilson. The latter gentleman (invariably known as *"Uncle Sam"*) generally superintended in person a large number of workmen, who on this occasion, were employed in overhauling the provisions purchased by the contractor for the army. The casks were marked E. A.—U. S. This work fell to the lot of a facetious fellow in the employ of the Messrs. Wilsons, who, on being asked by some of his fellow workmen the meaning of the mark, (for the letters U. S. for United States, was almost then entirely new to them) said "he did not know, unless it meant *Elbert Anderson and Uncle Sam"*—alluding exclusively, then, to the said "Uncle Sam" Wilson.

The joke caught on among Wilson's workers, who often teased him about "the increasing extent of his possessions." It quickly spread beyond Troy, an odd fate, the writer of this article noted, for a "silly joke."

Many aspects of the story check out: Thousands of troops were stationed just south of Troy, Anderson was a contractor for the government, and Wilson was a meat inspector with lots of nieces and nephews and others who called him Uncle Sam. The term clearly originated in upstate New York. Its first known appearance in a newspaper was in the Troy *Post* of September 7, 1813, and soon after it can also be found in Vermont newspapers near the Canadian frontier—where fighting was going on involving soldiers stationed near Troy.

Wilson's descendants had no doubts Sam Wilson was the original Uncle Sam. In 1917, the eighty-one-year-old Lucius Wilson stated that his great uncle was "the old original 'Uncle Sam,' who gave that name to the United States." Lucius Wilson added that his uncle was "jolly, genial,

generous" and married to Aunt Betsy. The evidence was sufficient to convince writer Alton Ketchum of the story's truth, and his 1959 study of the subject remains the most thorough. Adding to the story's appeal is that Samuel Wilson was born in what's now Arlington, Massachusetts, in a home right along Paul Revere's route from Boston to Lexington and Concord. Wilson was nine when Revere rode past.

The U. S. Congress came down firmly on the side of Sam Wilson. In September 1961, a joint resolution of the House and Senate resolved "that the Congress salutes 'Uncle Sam' Wilson, of Troy, New York, as the progenitor of America's national symbol of 'Uncle Sam.'"

Alas, there's reason for skepticism. As writer Albert Matthews pointed out in his 1908 book on the subject, many facts also militated against the story. First, the letters *U. S.* had stood for United States since early in the nineteenth century, and workmen in Troy ought not to have been perplexed by them. Second, none of Samuel Wilson's obituaries (he died in 1854) in Troy newspapers mentioned a connection to Uncle Sam (though the story did appear earlier in both Troy and Albany newspapers). Matthews proposed an alternate explanation: namely, that some unknown person had, for reasons equally unknown, extended the letters *U. S.* to "Uncle Sam."

Whatever its origins (and they remain uncertain), the image most of us have of Uncle Sam has nothing to do with Sam Wilson. In early cartoons, Uncle Sam has no single look; different artists give him different shapes. The first drawing of him did not appear until 1832, according to Ketchum. It portrayed "Uncle Sam in Danger" from Andrew Jackson, who has opened a vein in Sam's arm. The unknown artist was protesting Jackson's efforts to dismantle the Bank of the United States. This Uncle Sam was somewhat plump as well as sad. That same year, a pro-Jackson drawing depicted "Old Jack, the famous New Orleans mouser, clearing Uncle Sam's barn of bank and Clay rats." Jackson is a cat with a rat, possibly Henry Clay, in his mouth while Uncle Sam stands in the doorway of his barn saying "Bravo, my boys!" In an 1830s anti-Jackson cartoon, Uncle Sam is suffering from "La Grippe."

Uncle Sam in Danger (color print based on 1832 illustration). Harry T. Peters "America on Stone" Collection, National Museum of American History, Smithsonian Institution.

Old Jack, the Famous New Orleans Mouser... (1832). Library of Congress.

Uncle Sam Sick with La Grippe (1837). Library of Congress.

Out of One into Another from a drawing by Thomas Nast (1875). Library of Congress.

Some of Uncle Sam's early traits, such as his striped pants and whiskers, came from the portrayal in *Punch,* London's popular humor magazine, of an earlier American character called Brother Jonathan. Uncle Sam's beard probably stuck because of that of Abraham Lincoln, but it was Thomas Nast, a staff artist for *Harper's Weekly* famed for the cartoons that helped bring down Boss Tweed and his Tammany Hall political machine, who more than anyone gave us the image we still recognize as Uncle Sam. An 1875 Nast cartoon pictures Uncle Sam with what became his characteristic white whiskers, striped pants, long coat, and top hat. Sam is warning Republicans not to fall into the trap of a "reformed Tammany Hall." (Nast also helped create the modern image of Santa Claus.)

The most famous single image of Uncle Sam was drawn by James Montgomery Flagg. During the last two years of World War I, the government printed more than four million of his "I Want You for U.S. Army" posters. Flagg's Sam also appeared on a postage stamp. Uncle Sam has enlisted in every war since then, as well as numerous other causes.

How has he lived so long? For a nation that likes to think of itself as youthful and powerful, Sam seems too old, too clownish, too silly an image. But that may also have been part of his appeal. From the Revolution to the present, many of the most patriotic Americans have also been among those most suspicious of the powers of the U.S. government. A powerful father figure might have been more imposing but also more threatening. What Americans wanted, at least in their government, was not a stern father but an eccentric uncle.

I Want You for U.S. Army by James Montgomery Flagg (ca. 1917). Library of Congress.

THE MOST FAMILIAR IMAGE of George Washington, which has made it into everyone's wallet, comes from Gilbert Stuart's portrait. But though Stuart gave us Washington's face, it was Emanuel Leutze who gave us his heroism.

Leutze's painting *Washington Crossing the Delaware* portrays the night of Christmas 1776 when Washington led his beleaguered army through sleet and snow and across the icy Delaware River. The troops then marched to Trenton and surprised the Hessian mercenaries and continued to Princeton where they defeated the British.

"The image . . . is one of the folk-memories that most Americans share," wrote David Hackett Fischer in his masterful history of the campaign (to which this essay is greatly indebted). "In our mind's eye, we see a great river choked with ice, and a long line of little boats filled with horses, guns, and soldiers. In the foreground is the heroic figure of George Washington."

Washington's Crossings

Leutze peopled the boat with the flag-holding James Monroe and a range of American archetypes: riflemen, farmers, a seaman, a merchant, a Scottish immigrant, a black, even an androgynous figure who might be a woman. Above all, there is Washington: upright, determined, imposing. He is even more so when the painting is seen in person at New York's Metropolitan Museum of Art: Its actual size is roughly twelve feet high and twenty feet wide.

Unlike Stuart, for whom Washington posed, Leutze did not know Washington. Leutze was not born until 1816, seventeen years after Washington's death, and Leutze did not begin work on the painting until 1848. In fact, Leutze was not even in America at the time but rather in Germany, and his intent was at least as much to inspire supporters of the European revolutions of 1848 as it was to celebrate heroes of the American Revolution of 1776. This later led the *New York Times* to argue that the painting represented Washington crossing the Rhine, not the Delaware.

Such criticism was unfair. Leutze had lived in America and he drew heavily on American sources, among them Thomas Sully's 1819 painting *Passage of the Delaware* and a cast taken from the face of a statue of

Washington by Jean-Antoine Houdon. (Sully's painting also influenced Edward Hicks, a Quaker folk artist best known for his "Peaceable Kingdom" paintings, to create his own version of Washington's crossing.)

Leutze's efforts to make his *Crossing* fully American extended even to enlisting as models Americans visiting Düsseldorf. The only figure in the boat, according to Worthington Whittredge, a painter who was one of those who posed, who was not based on an American model was a Norwegian who was "acquainted with ice and accustomed to a boat and could be admitted."

Whittredge posed both as a steersman with an oar and as Washington himself. In his autobiography, Whittredge recalled Leutze's methods:

I stood two hours without moving, in order that the cloak of the Washington could be painted at a single sitting, thus enabling Leutze to catch the folds of the cloak as they were first arranged. Clad in Washington's full uniform, heavy chapeau and all, spy-glass in one hand and the other on my knee, I was nearly dead when the operation was over. They poured champagne down my throat and I lived through it.

Washington Crossing the Delaware by Emanuel Leutze (1851). Metropolitan Museum of Art, New York; gift of John Stewart Kennedy. Image source: Art Resource, NY.

The Passage of the Delaware by Thomas Sully (1819). Museum of Fine Arts, Boston; gift of the owners of the Old Boston Museum.

In 1850, just after Leutze finished the work, a fire in his studio caused severe damage, covering Washington and Monroe in a white haze. The painting was sufficiently restored to be displayed in the Bremen art museum until 1942, when the painting was destroyed by Royal Air Force bombing. Some, Fischer noted, saw this as Britain's "final act of retribution for the American Revolution."

Fortunately, soon after the fire in his studio Leutze painted another version, and it was this that made it to America in 1851. Here the artist's attention to his American sources and his awareness of the American sensibility paid off: The painting was an immediate hit. The *Bulletin of the American Art-Union* described it as "one of the greatest productions of the age, and eminently worthy to commemorate the grandest event in the military life of the illustrious man whom all nations delight to honor," and the New York *Evening Mirror* said it was "the grandest, most majestic, and most effective painting ever exhibited in America." Among those who saw the painting was the young Henry James, who later described how he "gaped responsive to every item, lost in the marvel of the wintry light, of the sharpness of the ice-blocks, of the sickness of the sick soldier . . . above all, of the profiled national hero's purpose, as might be said, of standing *up,* as much as possible, even indeed of doing it almost on one leg, in such difficulties, and successfully balancing."

So successful was Leutze's work that by the late nineteenth century Mark Twain, in *Life on the Mississippi,* commented that engravings could be found above the mantels in all the best homes along that river between St. Louis and Baton Rouge. Twain added that copies of the painting embroidered by the young ladies of those homes could be found on the walls by the doors and that these were works of art "which would have made Washington hesitate about crossing, if he could have foreseen what advantage was going to be taken of it."

Washington at the Delaware by Edward Hicks (1848–1849). The Colonial Williamsburg Foundation.

Washington Crossing the Delaware by George Caleb Bingham (1856–1871). Chrysler Museum of Art, Norfolk, Virginia; gift of Walter P. Chrysler Jr. in honor of Walter P. Chrysler Sr.

Leutze's painting also inspired more serious artists. George Caleb Bingham's 1871 *Washington Crossing the Delaware* moved the scene at least partly into his own century. Bingham placed the figures on a flatboat like those found on the Mississippi River, and he dressed many of those aboard in nineteenth-century frontier attire. Grant Wood's 1932 *Daughters of Revolution* placed three members of the Daughters of the American Revolution in front of Leutze's painting to represent how far they had strayed from its spirit. Larry Rivers's 1953 *Washington Crossing the Delaware,* featuring an off-center Washington and an anxious soldier, fit a period when artists saw heroism as out of fashion. Equally unheroic was Peter Saul's 1975 *Washington Crossing the Delaware,* in which the general is riding his trusty steed right into the river. Also in 1975, Robert Colescott's *George Washington Carver Crossing the Delaware* commented on American racism (as did, in its own way, an early twentieth-century postcard that eliminated the African American Leutze had placed on board).

(left) Washington Crossing the Delaware by Larry Rivers (1953). The Museum of Modern Art, New York. Art © Estate of Larry Rivers/Licensed by VAGA, New York, New York.

(below) Washington Crossing the Delaware by Peter Saul (1975). © Peter Saul. Private Collection, New York. Image courtesy of George Adams Gallery, New York.

Leutze's original had plenty of historical inaccuracies of its own. The boat and uniforms were wrong for the Continental army of 1776, horses and artillery were brought over separately, the crossing actually took place at night, the ice in the river was thinner than in the painting, and the Stars and Stripes held by Monroe was not adopted until 1777. Still, if Leutze's image was not entirely true to the details of history, it was surely true to its spirit. The situation

of Washington and his army in December 1776 was desperate. They had lost battle after battle, and many soldiers were preparing to give up and go home. Washington's crossing and his subsequent victories at Trenton and Princeton, historian James McPherson wrote, "saved the American Revolution from collapse." In crossing the river, Washington took a desperate gamble, and Leutze's painting captures the significance and drama of the moment.

LIBERTY AND COLUMBIA WERE DIGNIFIED and genteel ladies, appropriate for formal occasions where America took her place among other nations. They did not, however, fit the nation's image of itself as vigorous and virile, if a bit boorish. What was needed, in short, was a man.

The first popular male incarnation of America was Yankee Doodle, but he never had a generally recognized image. In 1778, the engraver Joseph Wright's *Yankee-Doodle, or the American Satan,* portrayed him as an ordinary young man, a bit glum but certainly not satanic, presumably because Wright, who lived in England but was born in America, wanted to mock British efforts to demonize Americans. That same year, a less sympathetic portrait, this from the British publisher Matthew Darly, showed Yankee Doodle celebrating the wounding of a black man. This Yankee Doodle, like the one in the song that made him famous, has stuck a feather in his cap.

Yankee Doodles and Brother Jonathans

In 1846, the artist Charles Martin gave him a top hat and an axe for the cover of a magazine named for him, but this was well after his heyday and there's no evidence anyone other than one particular artist thought this was the way he looked.

Yankee Doodle's name provides a few clues as to his looks. A doodle was a country bumpkin, and the Yankee Doodle of the song was a bit of a fool. He thought he could stick a feather in his cap and somehow take on the better-trained, better-armed, and better-dressed British army. Indeed, it was British troops who first marched to "Yankee Doodle," and that was to ridicule the Americans. The rebels appropriated the song while pushing back the British from Lexington and Concord. Since then, the *Pennsylvania Journal* of May 24, 1775, reported, *"Yankee Doodle* sounds less sweet to [British] ears."

Around 1825, plays started appearing featuring "Yankee" characters, offering literary historians further clues. In her study of American humor, Constance Rourke wrote that this Yankee "might be a peddler, a sailor, a Vermont wool-dealer, or merely a Green Mountain boy who traded and drawled and upset calculations." His costume was usually "a white bell-crowned hat, a coat with long tails that was usually blue, eccentric red and white trousers, and long boot-straps." Whatever he wore, he was sharp and

(left) *Yankee-Doodle, or the American Satan* by Joseph Wright (1778). Courtesy of the John Carter Brown Library at Brown University.

(below) *A View in America in 1778*, published by Matthew Darly (1778). The Colonial Williamsburg Foundation.

independent and absolutely certain he was the equal of anyone, especially anyone who thought himself superior.

By the 1830s, Yankee Doodle generally had been replaced by Brother Jonathan, another American everyman who at first seemed a fool but usually managed to make others look more foolish. Jonathan frequently appeared onstage and in cartoons, especially in the popular almanacs of the period.

The original Brother Jonathan, according to an 1846 account in the *Norwich (CT) Evening Courier,* was that state's former governor, Jonathan Trumbull. The newspaper attributed the following story to "a gentleman now upward of 80 years of age":

> When General Washington, after being appointed commander of the army of the Revolutionary War, came to Massachusetts to organize it, and make preparation for the defense of the country, he found a great destitution of ammunition and other means, necessary to meet the powerful foe he had to contend with, and great difficulty to obtain them. . . . On one occasion at that anxious period, a consultation of the officers and others was had, when it seemed no way could be devised to make such preparation as was necessary. His Excellency, Jonathan Trumbull, the elder, was then governor of the state of Connecticut, on whose judgement and aid the general placed the greatest reliance, and remarked, We must consult "Brother Jonathan" on the subject. The general did so, and the governor was successful in supplying many of the wants of the army. When difficulties after arose, and the army was spread over the country, it became a by-word, *"we must consult Brother Jonathan."* The term Yankee is still applied to a portion, but, *"Brother Jonathan"* has now become a designation of the whole country, as John Bull has, for England.

Horace Bushnell's 1851 history of Connecticut repeated the story, saying that "our Connecticut Jonathan was to Washington what the scripture Jonathan was to David, a true friend, a counsellor and stay of confidence— Washington's brother." In his 1859 biography of Trumbull, Isaac W. Stuart noted that Washington turned to Trumbull so frequently that the phrase "we must consult Brother Jonathan" spread throughout the army and then via soldiers returning home throughout the states until ultimately "it was universally appropriated, through its two emphatic closing words 'Brother

Jonathan,' as a sobriquet, current to the present day . . . for that mightiest of all republics that ever flung its standard to the breezes of heaven."

Other than the word of the unknown octogenarian, the Trumbull story is, alas, completely unsubstantiated. In his 1902 book on Brother Jonathan, Albert Matthews noted that neither Washington nor Trumbull ever alluded to the story and that there's no record of the story being told until 1846: forty-seven years after Washington's death, sixty-one years after Trumbull's death, and seventy-one years after Washington took command of the American forces.

The English & American Discovery . . . , published by Matthew Darly (1778). Courtesy of the John Carter Brown Library at Brown University.

More likely, Brother Jonathan may have been applied to Americans because his name was similar to that of John Bull, a common symbol of Britain. Jonathan's early appearances were often alongside John Bull. A 1778 print from Matthew Darly, *The English & American Discovery. Brother, Brother We Are Both in the Wrong,* presented the two together, as did the 1813 *Brother Jonathan Administering a Salutary Cordial to John Bull.*

Brother Jonathan Administering a Salutary Cordial to John Bull by Amos Doolittle (ca. 1813). Courtesy Winterthur Museum.

The two figures were also paired in James K. Paulding's popular 1812 *Diverting History of John Bull and Brother Jonathan.* As Paulding tells the story of Britain and America, "Bull's family had got to be so numerous that his farm was hardly large enough to portion them all with; so he sent his youngest son, Jonathan, or as he was familiarly called *Brother Jonathan,* to settle some new lands which he had on the other side of the mill-pond." Paulding described Jonathan as "a tall, stout, double-jointed, broad-footed cub of a fellow, awkward in his gait, and simple in his appearance; but shewing a lively, shrewd look, and having the promise of great strength when he should get his full growth." Paulding added that, despite Jonathan's odd looks, "every body that had seen John Bull, saw a great likeness between them, and swore that he was John's own boy."

Jonathan embodied the democratic rhetoric of the Jacksonian era. The embodiment of the common man, he is often pictured whittling. He may seem a hick, but he was supremely confident and competent. Alas, as literary historian Winifred Morgan chronicled his evolution, Jonathan's confidence gradually outstripped his humor. Perhaps this was partly because Americans no longer pictured themselves, even in jest, as country bumpkins. Perhaps, too, it was because by mid-century Jonathan was often downright racist. Instead of contrasting his exuberance to British affectations, artists increasingly portrayed Jonathan as the superior of immigrants and blacks. In 1855, for example, in *The Propagation Society. More Free Than Welcome,* the pope steps onto American shores demanding that Americans "kiss our big toe in token of submission." Jonathan will not submit to Catholicism or Catholic immigrants. Leaning against a flagpole, he answers: "No you dont, Mr. Pope!"

By this point, Jonathan has also come to look very much like Uncle Sam, and, though Sam generally represented the American government and Jonathan the average American or the nation as a whole, it was Sam's image and not Jonathan's that lasted.

*The Propagation Society. More Free
Than Welcome* by Nathaniel Currier
(ca. 1855). Library of Congress.

Notes for Quotes

Preface

5 "I wish the bald eagle had not been chosen"—Benjamin Franklin to Sarah Bache, 26 January 1784, unpublished volume 1783–1784, The Papers of Benjamin Franklin, digital edition, the Packard Humanities Institute, sponsored by the American Philosophical Society and Yale University, http://franklinpapers.org/franklin/framedVolumes.jsp.

5 "the inaccuracy of its drawing"—[Rembrandt Peale], *Portrait of Washington*, [prob. after 1825 and before 1832], Historical Society of Pennsylvania (call # Gw* .398 v.3), 7.

5 "The Revolution was in the minds and hearts of the people"—John Adams to Hezekiah Niles, 13 February 1818, in Charles Francis Adams, ed., *The Works of John Adams, Second President of the United States,* vol. 10 (Boston: Little, Brown, and Co., 1856), 282.

Declarations

6 "can read my name without spectacles"—John F. Watson, *Annals of Philadelphia and Pennsylvania, in the Olden Time; Being a Collection . . . ,* vol. 1 (n.p., 1843, 1850), 399.

6 "the [church] bells rang . . . cannon were discharged"—Abigail Adams to John Adams, 21 July 1776, Adams Family Papers: An Electronic Archive, Massachusetts Historical Society, http://www.masshist.org/digitaladams/aea/cfm/doc.cfm?id=L17760721aa.

8 "fairly engrossed [written by hand] on parchment" and "the Declaration of Independence being engrossed"—*Journals of the Continental Congress, 1774–1789,* vol. 5: June 5–October 8, 1776, ed. Worthington Chauncey Ford (Washington, DC: Government Printing Office, 1906), 590, 626.

9 "I have been constantly occupied"—John Trumbull to James Monroe, [29 December 1817], John Trumbull Papers, Manuscripts and Archives, Yale University Library.

10 "took the liberty of embellishing"—*Autobiography, Reminiscences and Letters of John Trumbull, from 1756 to 1841* (New York: Wiley and Putnam; New Haven, CT: Hamlen, 1841), 418.

10 "it is every way worthy"—*New York (NY) Gazette,* October 12, 1818.

10 "hand of time"—"Declaration of Independence: A History," from the online exhibition *The Charters of Freedom,* National Archives, http://www.archives.gov/exhibits/charters/declaration_history.html, accessed October 30, 2012.

Dollar Bills

12 "He was completely absorbed"—Jane Stuart, "The Youth of Gilbert Stuart," *Scribner's Monthly* (later *The Century Magazine*) 13, no. 5 (March 1877): 645.

12 "Sir Thomas Lawrence said"—Charles Robert Leslie, *Autobiographical Recollections* (Boston: Ticknor and Fields, 1860), 68.

12 "make a fortune" and "if I should be fortunate"—J. D. Herbert, *Irish Varieties, for the Last Fifty Years* (London: William Joy, 1836), 248.

14 "so sullen a mood"—George Washington to Dr. Boucher, 21 May 1772, in *The Writings of George Washington,* vol. 2, 1758–1775, ed. Worthington Chauncey Ford (New York: G. P. Putnam's Sons, 1889), 349.

14 "hundred-dollar bill"—George C. Mason, *The Life and Works of Gilbert Stuart* (New York: Charles Scribner's Sons, 1879), 106, 141.

14 "the expression of the countenance" and "the inaccuracy of its drawing"—Peale, *Portrait of Washington,* 7.

15 "All his features"—Isaac Weld Jr., *Travels Through the States of North America, and the Provinces of Upper and Lower Canada, during the Years 1795, 1796, and 1797,* 3rd ed., vol. 1 (London, 1800), 105–106.

15 "was less what Washington was"—John Neal, *Randolph,* vol. 2 (n.p., 1823), 63.

15 "His instinctive rightness of approach"—Richard McLanathan, *Gilbert Stuart* (New York: Abrams, 1986), 83.

15 "If George Washington should appear on earth"—Neal, *Randolph,* 64.

Eagles and Turkeys

16 "The eagle displayed"—E. T. Lander, "The Great Seal of the United States," *Magazine of American History* 29, no. 5 (May–June 1893): 480.

18 "I wish the bald eagle had not been chosen" and "Others object"—Franklin to Bache, 26 January 1784, unpublished volume 1783–1784, Papers of Benjamin Franklin, digital edition.

Fifes and Drums

20 "But a glance is needed"—*Cleveland (OH) Leader,* March 29, 1876.

20 "vile squealing"—*The Merchant of Venice,* Stephen Greenblatt, ed., *The Norton Shakespeare, Based on the Oxford Edition* (New York: Norton, 1997), 2.5.29.

20 "ear-piercing"—*Othello* (Greenblatt), 3.3.357.

20–21 "If buttercups buzz'd after the bee"—Barbara W. Tuchman, *The First Salute* (New York: Knopf, 1988), 288.

22 "a slow, melancholy air"—Richard M. Ketchum, *Victory at Yorktown: The Campaign That Won the Revolution* (New York: Henry Holt, 2004), 249.

23 "appeared to be much in liquor"—*The Journal of Lieut. William Feltman, of the First Pennsylvania Regiment, 1781–82 . . .* (Philadelphia, 1853), 22.

23 "The English marched out"—Jared Sparks Collection of American Manuscripts, 1582–1843 (MS Sparks 32, p. 248). Houghton Library, Harvard University.

Kites and Caps

24 "double spectacles"—*The Works of Benjamin Franklin; Containing Several Political and Historical Tracts . . . ,* vol. 10, ed. Jared Sparks (Boston: Hilliard, Gray, and Co., 1840), 178.

24 "Provide a small iron rod"—Benjamin Franklin, *Poor Richard's Almanack* (New York: Barnes and Noble Publishing, 2004; originally published 1733–1758), 228.

26 "Surely the thunder of heaven"—Benjamin Franklin to Cadwallader Colden, 12 April 1753, in *The Papers of Benjamin Franklin,* vol. 4: July 1, 1750, through June 30, 1753, ed. Leonard W. Labaree (New Haven, CT: Yale University Press, 1961), 463.

26 "His name was familiar"—*The Works of John Adams, Second President of the United States . . . ,* vol. 1, ed. Charles Francis Adams (Boston: Little, Brown and Co., 1856), 660.

26 "that the French had read Rousseau"—Walter Isaacson, "What Benjamin Franklin Means for Our Times," in Page Talbott, ed., *Benjamin Franklin in Search of a Better World* (New Haven, CT: Yale University Press, 2005), 9.

26 "Figure me"—Benjamin Franklin to Mrs. Thompson, 8 February 1777, in *The Works of Dr. Benjamin Franklin, in Philosophy, Politics, and Morals . . . ,* vol. 6, ed. William Temple Franklin (Philadelphia, 1809), 83.

27 "for everyone to have an engraving"—As quoted in Gordon S. Wood, *The Americanization of Benjamin Franklin* (New York: Penguin Press, 2004), 177.

27 "He snatched the lightning from the skies"—As quoted in J. A. Leo Lemay, "The Life of Benjamin Franklin," in Talbott, *Benjamin Franklin in Search of a Better World,* 46.

27 "have made your father's face"—Benjamin Franklin to Sarah Bache, 3 June 1779, in *The Papers of Benjamin Franklin,* vol. 29, March 1–June 30, 1779, ed. Barbara B. Oberg (New Haven, CT: Yale University Press, 1992), 613.

27 "sat so much and so often"—Benjamin Franklin to Thomas Digges, 25 June [1780], in *The Papers of Benjamin Franklin,* vol. 32, March 1–June 30, 1780, ed. Barbara B. Oberg (New Haven, CT: Yale University Press, 1996), 590.

Lady Liberties

31 "At that time my Statue of Liberty did not exist"—As quoted in Andre Gschaedler, *True Light on the Statue of Liberty and Its Creator* (Narberth, PA: Livingston Publishing Co., 1966), 15.

31 "If I myself felt that spirit here"—As quoted in Neil G. Kotler, "The Statue of Liberty as Idea, Symbol, and Historical Presence" in *The Statue of Liberty Revisited,* ed. Wilton S. Dillon and Neil G. Kotler (Washington, DC: Smithsonian Institution Press, 1994), 10.

32 "The workshop was built"—As quoted in "The Colossus of New York," *Boston Evening Transcript,* August 14, 1878.

33 "We will not forget"—Grover Cleveland, *The Public Papers of Grover Cleveland, March 4, 1885, to March 4, 1889* (Washington: Government Printing Office, 1889), 177.

33 "Mother of Exiles" and "'Give me your tired, your poor'"—Emma Lazarus, "The New Colossus" in *The Poems of Emma Lazarus,* vol. 1 (Boston: Houghton, Mifflin and Co., 1888), 202–203.

33 "If you are going to make this island"—*Judge* 17, no. 440 (March 22, 1890): cover.

Liberty Bells

34 "In yonder wooden steeple"—George Lippard, *Legends of the American Revolution; or, Washington and His Generals* (Philadelphia: T. B. Peterson and Brothers, 1847), 391–392.

35 "they are much incommoded"—Pennsylvania Archives, Eighth Series, vol. 8, January 7, 1771–September 26, 1776, ed. Charles F. Hoban, 1935, p. 6856.

35, 37 "We were working away"—*New York Times,* July 16, 1911.

37 "I had the mortification"—Isaac Norris to Robert Charles, 10 March 1753, as quoted in Charles Michael Boland, *Ring in the Jubilee: The Epic of America's Liberty Bell* (Riverside, CT: Chatham Press, 1973), 41.

37 *"The old Independence Bell"*—*Public Ledger* (Philadelphia), February 26, 1846.

37 "We Got a Lemon" and "What about the Warranty?"—"The Story of the Liberty Bell," Whitechapel Bell Foundry Ltd., http://www.whitechapelbellfoundry.co.uk/liberty.htm, accessed October 30, 2012.

37 "Liberty Bell"—"The Liberty Bell," *Anti-Slavery Record* 1, no. 2 (February 1835): 23.

38 "The Liberty Bell sounded freedom"—*Deseret Evening News* (Salt Lake City, UT), July 12, 1915.

38 "Now it is truly everyone's bell"—Gary B. Nash, *The Liberty Bell* (New Haven, CT: Yale University Press, 2010), 217.

Liberty Trees

40 "decorated in a splendid manner"—*Boston Gazette,* May 19, 1766.

42 "From the east to the west"—*Pennsylvania Magazine: or, American Monthly Museum* 1 (July 1775): 328.

42 "the tree of liberty must be refreshed"—Thomas Jefferson to William Stephens Smith, 13 November 1787, in *The Papers of Thomas Jefferson Digital Edition,* ed. Barbara B. Oberg and J. Jefferson Looney (Charlottesville: University of Virginia Press, Rotunda, 2008), http://rotunda.upress.virginia.edu/founders/TSJN-01-12-02-0348, accessed October 29, 2012.

Massacres

44 "an unhappy disturbance"—*A Fair Account of the Late Unhappy Disturbance at Boston in New England . . .* (London, 1770), title page.

44 "that he did not blame"—*The Trial of William Wemms, James Hartegan, William McCauley, Hugh White, Matthew Killroy, William Warren, John Carrol, and Hugh Montgomery, Soldiers in His Majesty's 29th Regiment of Foot . . . ,* trans. John Hodgson (Boston; reprint London, [1771?]), 125.

47 "I thought I had entrusted"—Henry Pelham to Paul Revere, 29 March 1770, in *Letters and Papers of John Singleton Copley and Henry Pelham, 1739–1776,* Collections of the Massachusetts Historical Society 71 (Boston: Massachusetts Historical Society, 1914), 83.

47 "an original print"—See, for example, *Boston Gazette, and Country Journal,* April 2, 1770.

Pyramids and Eyes

48 "the 18th day of September"—See, for example, *Bartgis's Maryland Gazette, and Frederick-Town Weekly Advertiser,* September 25, 1793.

50 "They are in general a very harmless sort of people"—Franklin to Josiah and Abiah Franklin, 13 April 1738, in *The Papers of Benjamin Franklin,* vol. 2: January 1, 1735–December 31, 1744, ed. Leonard W. Labaree (New Haven, CT: Yale University Press, 1960), 204.

51 "The pyramid signifies strength"—*Journals of the Continental Congress, 1774–1789,* vol. 22: January 1–August 9, 1782, ed. Gaillard Hunt (Washington, DC: Government Printing Office, 1914), 339–340.

51 "It seems likely"—Richard S. Patterson and Richardson Dougall, *The Eagle and the Shield: A History of the Great Seal of the United States* (Washington, DC: Office of the Historian, Department of State, 1976), 532.

51 "In 1934"—Henry Wallace to Dal Lee, 6 February 1951, Henry A. Wallace Papers, Correspondence, February 1951–August 1952, reel #48, frame #17, University of Iowa, Libraries, Special Collections.

Snakes

52 "A plan for the union"—*The Autobiography of Benjamin Franklin* (Philadelphia: Henry Altemus, 1895), 230.

52 "'Tis true, that the arms"—*Rivington's New-York (NY) Gazetteer,* January 19, 1775.

52 "The dragon represented Greatbritain"—Isaiah Thomas, *The History of Printing in America . . . ,* vol. 2 (Worcester, Eng., 1810), 252.

52 "United now alive and free"—*New-York (NY) Journal; or, The General Advertiser,* December 15, 1774.

54 "Don't tread on me"—See, for example, Dixon and Hunter's *Virginia Gazette* (Williamsburg), May 11, 1776.

54 "To those familiar with the Judeo-Christian tradition"—Lester C. Olson, *Emblems of American Community in the Revolutionary Era: A Study in Rhetorical Iconology* (Washington, DC: Smithsonian Institution Press, 1991), xiii.

54 "the snake ye with wonder behold"—*Massachusetts Spy or, Thomas's Boston Journal,* September 15, 1774.

55 "never begins an attack" and "the Rattle-Snake is found in no other quarter"—*Pennsylvania Journal; and the Weekly Advertiser* (Philadelphia), December 27, 1775.

Stars and Stripes

56 "a signal of submission" and "by this time"—George Washington to Lieutenant Colonel Joseph Reed, 4 January 177[6], in *The Papers of George Washington Digital Edition,* ed. Theodore J. Crackel (Charlottesville: University of Virginia Press, Rotunda, 2008), http://rotunda.upress.virginia.edu/founders /GEWN-03-03-02-0016, accessed October 30, 2012.

56 "that the flag"—*Journals of the Continental Congress, 1774–1789,* vol. 8: May 22–October 2, 1777, ed. Worthington Chauncey Ford (Washington, DC: Government Printing Office, 1907), 464.

58 "devices for the Continental currency," "the flag of the United States of America," "a quarter cask of the public wine," and "be a proper and reasonable reward"—Francis Hopkinson to the Board of Admiralty, undated, Papers of Paymaster Pierce, Papers of the Continental Congress, National Archives and Records Administration, M247, record group 360, item no. 62, p. 577.

58 "sundry devices" and "the great naval flag"—Francis Hopkinson Account, 6 June 1780, Papers of Paymaster Pierce, Papers of the Continental Congress, National Archives and Records Administration, M247, record group 360, item no. 62, p. 579.

58 "was not the only person"—*Journals of the Continental Congress, 1774–1789,* vol. 18: September 7–December 29, 1780, ed. Gaillard Hunt (Washington, DC: Government Printing Office, 1910), 984.

60 "Washington was a frequent visitor"—George Henry Preble, *Our Flag: Origin and Progress of the Flag of the United States of America . . .* (Albany, NY: Joel Munsell, 1872), 193–194.

61 "The Betsy Ross story served" and "a strong-willed woman"—Marc Leepson, *Flag: An American Biography* (New York: St. Martin's Press, 2005), 43.

61 "hinged not just on eloquent political rhetoric"—Marla R. Miller, *Betsy Ross and the Making of America* (New York: Henry Holt, 2010), 15.

Uncle Sams

62 "Immediately after the declaration," "the increasing extent," and "silly joke"—[Sholto Percy and Reuben Percy], *The Percy Anecdotes, Revised Edition. To Which Is Added a Valuable Collection of American Anecdotes,* vol. 2 (New York: J. & J. Harper, 1832), 76.

62, 64 "the old original 'Uncle Sam'" and "jolly, genial, generous"—Rutherford Hayner, *Troy and Rensselaer County, New York: A History,* vol. 1 (New York: Lewis Historical Publishing Co., 1925), 177.

64 "that the Congress salutes"—*United States Statutes at Large . . . ,* vol. 75 (Washington, DC: U. S. Government Printing Office, 1961), 966.

Washington's Crossings

68 "The image . . . is one of the folk-memories"—David Hackett Fischer, *Washington's Crossing* (New York: Oxford University Press, 2004), 1.

69 "acquainted with ice"—*The Autobiography of Worthington Whittredge, 1820–1910,* ed. John I. H. Baur (New York: Arno, 1942), 23.

69 "I stood two hours"—Ibid., 22.

70 "final act of retribution"—Fischer, *Washington's Crossing,* 3.

70 "one of the greatest productions"—"Opening of the Autumn Exhibition," *Bulletin of the American Art-Union,* no. 7 (October 1, 1851): 116.

70–71 "the grandest, most majestic"—*Evening Mirror* (New York, NY), November 7, 1851, as quoted in Raymond L. Stehle, "Washington Crossing the Delaware," *Pennsylvania History* 31, no. 3 (July 1964): 279.

71 "gaped responsive"—Henry James, *A Small Boy and Others: A Critical Edition,* ed. Peter Collister (Charlottesville: University of Virginia Press, 2011), 208.

71 "which would have made Washington hesitate"—Mark Twain, *Life on the Mississippi* (New York: Harper & Brothers, 1901), 279.

73 "saved the American Revolution"—Editor's note in Fischer, *Washington's Crossing,* ix.

Yankee Doodles and Brother Jonathans

74 "*Yankee Doodle* sounds less sweet"—*Pennsylvania Journal; and the Weekly Advertiser* (Philadelphia), May 24, 1775.

74 "might be a peddler" and "a white bell-crowned hat"—Constance Rourke, *American Humor: A Study of the National Character* (New York: Harcourt, Brace, 1931; New York: New York Review of Books, 2004), 25.

76 "a gentleman now upward" and "When General Washington, after being appointed commander"—*Norwich (CT) Evening Courier,* November 12, 1846.

76 "our Connecticut Jonathan was to Washington"—Horace Bushnell, *Speech for Connecticut: Being an Historical Estimate of the State, Delivered before the Legislature and Other Invited Guests . . .* (Hartford, CT: Boswell and Faxon, 1851), 34.

76–77 "it was universally appropriated"—I[saac] W[illiam] Stuart, *Life of Jonathan Trumbull Sen., Governor of Connecticut* (Boston, MA: Crocker and Brewster, 1859), 697.

77 "Bull's family had got to be so numerous," "a tall, stout, double-jointed, broad-footed cub," and "every body that had seen John Bull" [James K. Paulding], *The Diverting History of John Bull and Brother Jonathan* (New York, 1812), 4–5, 6–7.

Additional illustration credits

27 Duplessis, Joseph-Siffred (1725–1802). Consignment : COA0094822 (Position : 2) Benjamin Franklin (1706–1790). 1778. Oil on canvas, Oval, 28½ x 23 in. (72.4 x 58.4 cm). The Friedsam Collection, Bequest of Michael Friedsam, 1931 (32.100.132). The Metropolitan Museum of Art, New York, NY, U.S.A. Image copyright © The Metropolitan Museum of Art. Image source: Art Resource, NY.

69 Leutze, Emanuel Gottlieb (1816–1868). Consignment : COA0094822 (Position : 1) Washington Crossing the Delaware. 1851. Oil on canvas, 149 x 255 in. (378.5 x 647.7 cm). Gift of John Stewart Kennedy, 1897 (97.34). The Metropolitan Museum of Art, New York, NY, U.S.A. Image copyright © The Metropolitan Museum of Art. Image source: Art Resource, NY.

BACK COVER The Great Seal of the United States, lithograph by Andrew B. Graham (prob. 1885–1900). Library of Congress.

Bibliography

General

Fischer, David Hackett. *Liberty and Freedom*. New York: Oxford University Press, 2005.

Young, Alfred F., and Terry J. Fife with Mary E. Janzen. *We the People: Voices and Images of the New Nation*. Philadelphia: Temple University Press, 1993.

Declarations

Cooper, Helen A. *John Trumbull: The Hand and Spirit of a Painter*. New Haven, CT: Yale University Art Gallery, 1982.

"Declaration of Independence: A History." *The Charters of Freedom*. National Archives. http://www.archives.gov/exhibits/charters/declaration_history.html, accessed October 30, 2012.

Jaffe, Irma B. *Trumbull. The Declaration of Independence*. London: Allen Lane, 1976.

Maier, Pauline. *American Scripture: Making the Declaration of Independence*. New York: Alfred A. Knopf, 1997.

Wills, Garry. *Inventing America: Jefferson's Declaration of Independence*. Garden City, NY: Doubleday, 1978.

Dollar Bills

Chernow, Ron. *Washington: A Life*. New York: Penguin, 2010.

Evans, Dorinda. *The Genius of Gilbert Stuart*. Princeton, NJ: Princeton University Press, 1999.

Flexner, James Thomas. *On Desperate Seas: A Biography of Gilbert Stuart*. New York: Fordham University Press, 1995.

McLanathan, Richard. *Gilbert Stuart*. New York: Harry N. Abrams in association with the National Museum of American Art, Smithsonian Institution, 1986.

Miller, Lillian B. *In Pursuit of Fame: Rembrandt Peale, 1778–1860*. Washington, DC: National Portrait Gallery, Smithsonian Institution in association with the University of Washington Press, 1992.

Mount, Charles Merrill. *Gilbert Stuart: A Biography*. New York: W. W. Norton, 1964.

National Gallery of Art. *Gilbert Stuart: Portraitist of the Young Republic, 1755–1828*. Providence, RI: Museum of Art, Rhode Island School of Design, 1967.

Eagles and Turkeys

Lemay, J. A. Leo. "The American Aesthetic of Franklin's Visual Creations." *Pennsylvania Magazine of History and Biography* 111, no. 4 (October 1987): 465–499.

Olson, Lester C. *Benjamin Franklin's Vision of American Community: A Study in Rhetorical Iconology*. Columbia: University of South Carolina Press, 2004.

Olson, Lester C. *Emblems of American Community in the Revolutionary Era: A Study in Rhetorical Iconology*. Washington, DC: Smithsonian Institution Press, 1991.

Patterson, Richard S., and Richardson Dougall. *The Eagle and the Shield: A History of the Great Seal of the United States*. Washington, DC: Office of the Historian, Department of State, 1976.

Sommer, Frank H. "Emblem and Device: The Origin of the Great Seal of the United States."
	Art Quarterly 24, no. 1 (Spring 1961): 57–76.

U. S. Department of State, Bureau of Public Affairs. *The Great Seal of the United States.*
	Washington, DC: U. S. Department of State, 2003.

Fifes and Drums

Camus, Raoul F. *Military Music of the American Revolution.* Chapel Hill: University of North
	Carolina Press, 1976.

Chandler, Eric Alan. *A History of Rudimental Drumming in America from the Revolutionary War
	to the Present.* Ann Arbor, MI: University Microfilms International, 1991.

Gordon, Willard F. *"The Spirit of '76" . . . an American Portrait: America's Best Known Painting,
	Least Known Artist.* Fallbrook, CA: Quail Hill Associates, 1976.

Greene, Jerome A. *The Guns of Independence: The Siege of Yorktown, 1781.* New York: Savas
	Beatie, 2005.

Ketchum, Richard M. *Victory at Yorktown: The Campaign That Won the Revolution.* New York:
	Henry Holt, 2004.

Moon, John C. "Some Questions (and a Few Answers) about British Military Music Lineage from
	Earlier Century Sources." Unpublished manuscript in John D. Rockefeller, Jr. Library,
	Williamsburg, VA, 2003.

Tuchman, Barbara W. *The First Salute.* New York: Alfred A. Knopf, 1988.

White, William Carter. *A History of Military Music in America.* New York: Exposition Press, 1944.
	Reprint, Westport, CT: Greenwood, 1975.

Kites and Caps

Gaustad, Edwin S. *Benjamin Franklin.* New York: Oxford University Press, 2006.

Isaacson, Walter. *Benjamin Franklin: An American Life.* New York: Simon and Schuster, 2003.

Talbott, Page, ed. *Benjamin Franklin in Search of a Better World.* New Haven, CT: Yale University
	Press, 2005.

Wood, Gordon S. *The Americanization of Benjamin Franklin.* New York: Penguin, 2004.

Lady Liberties

Dillon, Wilton S., and Neil G. Kotler, eds. *The Statue of Liberty Revisited.* Washington, DC:
	Smithsonian Institution Press, 1994.

Fox, Nancy Jo. *Liberties with Liberty: The Fascinating History of America's Proudest Symbol.* New York:
	E. P. Dutton in association with the Museum of American Folk Art, 1986.

Handlin, Oscar, and the editors of the Newsweek Book Division. *Statue of Liberty.* New York:
	Newsweek, 1971.

Shapiro, Mary J. *Gateway to Liberty: The Story of the Statue of Liberty and Ellis Island.* New York:
	Vintage, 1986.

Trachtenberg, Marvin. *The Statue of Liberty.* London: Allen Lane, 1976.

Liberty Bells

Independence Hall Association. "The Liberty Bell." www.ushistory.org/libertybell, accessed
	October 30, 2012.

Mires, Charlene. *Independence Hall in American Memory*. Philadelphia: University of Pennsylvania Press, 2002.

Nash, Gary B. *The Liberty Bell*. New Haven, CT: Yale University Press, 2010.

Rosewater, Victor. *The Liberty Bell: Its History and Significance*. New York: D. Appleton, 1926.

Voorhis, Harold V. B., and Ronald E. Heaton. *Loud and Clear: The Story of Our Liberty Bell*. Norristown, PA: Ronald E. Heaton, 1970.

Whitechapel Bell Foundry Ltd. "The Story of the Liberty Bell." http://www.whitechapelbellfoundry .co.uk/liberty.htm, accessed October 30, 2012.

Liberty Trees

Schlesinger, Arthur M. "Liberty Tree: A Genealogy." *New England Quarterly* 25, no. 4 (December 1952): 435–458.

Young, Alfred F. *Liberty Tree: Ordinary People and the American Revolution*. New York: New York University Press, 2006.

Massacres

Brigham, Clarence S. *Paul Revere's Engravings*. New York: Atheneum, 1969.

Fischer, David Hackett. *Paul Revere's Ride*. New York: Oxford University Press, 1994.

Forbes, Esther. *Paul Revere and the World He Lived In*. Boston: Houghton Mifflin, 1942.

Wroth, L. Kinvin, and Hiller B. Zobel, eds. *Legal Papers of John Adams*. Vol. 3, *Cases 63 and 64: The Boston Massacre Trials*. Cambridge, MA: Belknap Press, 1965.

Zobel, Hiller B. *The Boston Massacre*. New York: Norton, 1970.

Pyramids and Eyes

Bullock, Steven C. *Revolutionary Brotherhood: Freemasonry and the Transformation of the American Social Order, 1730–1840*. Chapel Hill: University of North Carolina Press, 1996.

Patterson, Richard S., and Richardson Dougall. *The Eagle and the Shield: A History of the Great Seal of the United States*. Washington, DC: Office of the Historian, Department of State, 1976.

Ridley, Jasper. *The Freemasons: A History of the World's Most Powerful Secret Society*. New York: Arcade, 2001.

Tabbert, Mark A. *American Freemasons: Three Centuries of Building Communities*. Lexington, MA: National Heritage Museum; New York: New York University Press, 2005.

U. S. Department of State, Bureau of Public Affairs. *The Great Seal of the United States*. Washington, DC: U. S. Department of State, 2003.

Snakes

Dolmetsch, Joan D. *Rebellion and Reconciliation: Satirical Prints on the Revolution at Williamsburg*. Williamsburg, VA: Colonial Williamsburg Foundation, 1976.

Olson, Lester C. *Emblems of American Community in the Revolutionary Era: A Study in Rhetorical Iconology*. Washington, DC: Smithsonian Institution Press, 1991.

Stars and Stripes

Furlong, William Rea, and Byron McCandless. *So Proudly We Hail: The History of the United States Flag*. Washington, DC: Smithsonian Institution Press, 1981.

Guenter, Scot M. *The American Flag, 1777–1924: Cultural Shifts from Creation to Codification.* Rutherford, NJ: Fairleigh Dickinson University Press, 1990.

Leepson, Marc. *Flag: An American Biography.* New York: Thomas Dunne Books, 2005.

Miller, Marla R. *Betsy Ross and the Making of America.* New York: Henry Holt, 2010.

Quaife, Milo M., Melvin J. Weig, and Roy E. Appleman. *The History of the United States Flag: From the Revolution to the Present, Including a Guide to Its Use and Display.* New York: Harper & Brothers, 1961.

Uncle Sams

Horwitz, Elinor Lander. *The Bird, the Banner, and Uncle Sam: Images of America in Folk and Popular Art.* Philadelphia: J. B. Lippincott, 1976.

Ketchum, Alton. *Uncle Sam: The Man and the Legend.* New York: Hill and Wang, 1959.

Matthews, Albert. *Uncle Sam.* Worcester, MA: Davis Press, 1908.

Washington's Crossings

Fischer, David Hackett. *Washington's Crossing.* New York: Oxford University Press, 2004.

Groseclose, Barbara S. *Emanuel Leutze, 1816–1868: Freedom Is the Only King.* Washington, DC: Smithsonian Institution Press, 1975.

Spassky, Natalie. *American Paintings in the Metropolitan Museum of Art.* Vol. 2, *A Catalogue of Works by Artists Born between 1816 and 1845.* New York: Metropolitan Museum of Art, 1985.

Stehle, Raymond L. "Washington Crossing the Delaware." *Pennsylvania History* 31, no. 3 (July 1964): 269–294.

Weekley, Carolyn J. *The Kingdoms of Edward Hicks.* Williamsburg, VA: Colonial Williamsburg Foundation in association with Harry N. Abrams, 1999.

Yankee Doodles and Brother Jonathans

Fleming, E. McClung. "Symbols of the United States: From Indian Queen to Uncle Sam." In *Frontiers of American Culture,* edited by Ray B. Browne, Richard H. Crowder, Virgil L. Lokke, and William T. Stafford, 1–24. West Lafayette, IN: Purdue University Studies, 1968.

Ketchum, Alton. *Uncle Sam: The Man and the Legend.* New York: Hill and Wang, 1959.

Matthews, Albert. *Brother Jonathan.* Cambridge, MA: John Wilson and Son, 1902.

Morgan, Winifred. *An American Icon: Brother Jonathan and American Identity.* Newark: University of Delaware Press, 1988.

Sonneck, Oscar George Theodore. *Report on "The Star-Spangled Banner," "Hail Columbia," "America," "Yankee Doodle."* New York: Dover, 1972. Originally published by the Library of Congress in 1909.

Index

Note: Page numbers for illustrations are shown in **bold.**

About Colonial Williamsburg

The Colonial Williamsburg Foundation is the not-for-profit center for history and citizenship, encouraging audiences at home and around the world to learn from the past.

Colonial Williamsburg is dedicated to the preservation, restoration, and presentation of eighteenth-century Williamsburg and the study, interpretation, and teaching of America's founding principles. In the Revolutionary City, the 301-acre restored eighteenth-century capital of Virginia, we interpret the origins of the idea of America.

The Foundation actively supports history and citizenship education through a wide variety of outreach programs. These include Electronic Field Trips, which transport the story of our nation to students across the country; the Colonial Williamsburg Teacher Institute, which immerses elementary, middle, and high school teachers in interdisciplinary approaches to history and government; and *The Idea of America*™, a digital, interactive learning experience that brings American history to life and invites participants to look at history through the lens of key American values.

About the Author

Paul Aron is director of Publications at the Colonial Williamsburg Foundation. His previous books include *We Hold These Truths . . . And Other Words That Made America.*

Acknowledgments

I am grateful for the assistance of my colleagues and former colleagues at the Colonial Williamsburg Foundation: Laura Barry, Shanin Glenn, Erik Goldstein, Angelika Kuettner, Doug Mayo, Helen Olds, Lou Powers, Sherri Powers, Amy Watson, Carolyn Weekley, and Bill White.